Books To Look Out
By Abraham S. Raj

Apostolic and Prophetic Handbook Series:
(the God wants you to ... series)

> Vol. 1 *Prophetic Handbook: God Wants You to Prophesy (Five Steps to Get You Prophesying)*
>
> Vol. 2 *Deliverance Handbook: God Wants You to Cast out Demons and Live Demon Free*
>
> Vol. 3 *Healing Handbook: God Wants You to Heal the Sick and Live in Healing*
>
> Vol. 4 *Prosperity Handbook: God Wants You to Prosper and Prosper Others*
>
> Vol. 5 *Signs and Wonders Handbook: God Wants You to Move in Signs and Wonders*

Apostolic and Prophetic Dictionary: Language of the End-Time Church (**Now available and sold separately**)

Equipped, Activated, and Released Series (**TEAR Programme**)

> Vol. 1 *Believer's Handbook*
> Vol. 2 *Leader's Handbook*
> Vol. 3 *Minister's Handbook*

Visit our website to check out what is currently available and more great resources like CDs, DVDs, and free materials.

www.kingspriests.co.za

God Wants You to Prophesy
5 Steps to Get You Prophesying
(Prophetic Handbook)

For you can all prophesy ... (1 Cor. 14:31)

Abraham S Rajah

WestBow
P R E S S
A DIVISION OF THOMAS NELSON

WestBow Press books may be ordered through booksellers or by contacting:

WestBow Press
A Division of Thomas Nelson
1663 Liberty Drive
Bloomington, IN 47403
www.westbowpress.com
1 (866) 928-1240

Because of the dynamic nature of the Internet, any web addresses or links contained
in this book may have changed since publication and may no longer be valid. The views
expressed in this work are solely those of the author and do not necessarily reflect the
views of the publisher, and the publisher hereby disclaims any responsibility for them.

Any people depicted in stock imagery provided by Thinkstock are models,
and such images are being used for illustrative purposes only.
Certain stock imagery © Thinkstock.

Scripture taken from the New King James Version. Copyright 1979, 1980,
1982 by Thomas Nelson, inc. Used by permission. All rights reserved.

ISBN: 978-1-4908-1914-3 (sc)

Library of Congress Control Number: 2013922077

Printed in the United States of America.

WestBow Press rev. date: 2/17/2014

Dedication

This book is dedicated first to the one true God, my Father, Saviour, and Comforter. You are everything to me. I am all I am and still to become because of You.

I also give a special dedication to my wife and inspiration, Hephzibah, who lovingly allowed me to take time off my legal practice to produce this book while she worked on cases alone. (*You always were a better lawyer.*) I love you, sweetheart. Thank you for making the love of God real to me.

To my three angels, Abigail, Elijah, and Zion Abraham, Daddy loves you and has seen a glimpse of the Father's grace through you.

CONTENTS

PART 1
INTRODUCTION TO THE PROPHETIC MINISTRY

PART 2
THE FIVE STEPS TO GET YOU PROPHESYING

PART 3
A WORD TO PASTORS AND LEADERS

PART 4
EXTRACTS FROM *THE APOSTOLIC*
AND PROPHETIC DICTIONARY

Acknowledgments

To everyone who supported me.
To Aps Motumi and my wife for proofreading.
To Rodney Reddy for indexing and editing.
Thank you all so much.

FOREWORD

This book is a must read for all who desire to hear God's voice and move in the prophetic ministry. It is simple yet deep and precise.

It is relevant to both the beginner and the experienced believer. It will help you deliver God's prophetic word accurately and precisely in such a way that the prophetic will be attractive to others.

For everyone who desires to hear God's voice and bless others through the prophetic, know for sure that you have done well to get your hands on this book. God is moving in these last days, and He wants all believers to partake in what He is doing on the earth. The Holy Spirit is training believers to move in apostolic signs, wonders, and miracles and in the prophetic ministry, and He desires all believers to move in them.

This book will help you to be in the present move of God and be a vessel of honour in God's hand.

Mufaro Maposa
Apostle, Prophet, and Founder
(Manifest Sons of God Movement)

PREFACE

Why a Book on the Prophetic Ministry?

The answer to the above question is because there is a lack of clear and simple teaching on this subject. Therefore the teaching in this book has been prepared *first* to help you realize that God wants you to move in the prophetic ministry and *second* to teach you how to move in it.

God instructed me to write this book because God is raising the church and believers to a level where *we can all receive prophetic messages for ourselves and for others* (1 Cor. 12:7). So whether you have never prophesied before or have done so every once in a while, this book will ignite and activate the prophetic gifts in you and move you to the next level of your walk with the Holy Spirit.

How to Use This Book

This book can be used by individuals in home cells meetings, training centres, Bible schools, and church services. At the end of each chapter, you will find three categories of activities:

> **Reflections:** These are extracts taken from the book for you to reflect on to make sure you have received most of what the chapter has to offer.

Exercise: These are some exercises that will help get the prophetic flow in you going.

Prayer: Here I join my faith with yours as we enforce our biblical privilege and right to answered prayer in the name of Jesus and by the power of the Holy Spirit on a specific subject according to what is contained in the chapter.

I encourage you to take the principles you will learn in this book seriously by studying them in a prayerful manner with your Bible, pen, and notebook. If you are serious about the prophetic ministry, it will definitely flow through you. *The anointing you respect is the anointing you will attract.*

My prayer is that as you read this book, God will open the rivers of living water inside you to flow like a mighty river until the river impacts your life and those around you with the prophetic ministry.

Please write, text, or e-mail us about the impact of this book in your life. I would love to hear from you. *(Contact information on the last pages.)*

In His Love,

Apostle and Prophet Abraham S. Rajah

PART 1

Introduction to the Prophetic Ministry

CHAPTER 1

Introduction

What Is The Prophetic?

The word *prophetic* can refer to all the ways in which God communicates His heart and mind in and through people.

You will learn that God communicates in many ways but only has one intention for His message: to fulfil His plans on the earth.

What Is the Prophetic Ministry?

The word *ministry* simply means service, so to minister means to serve. Every one of us is a minister or servant of the Lord Jesus Christ. This word must not be limited to preachers because all believers are ministers in one way or another.

The word *prophetic* comes from the root word *prophet* or *prophesies*. In the New Testament, it is the Greek word *propheteuo*, which means "to speak divinely or by inspiration from God." In other words, it refers to the Holy Spirit partnering with an individual to make known plans ordained from eternity past. God has a plan for every believer—a good plan—and He reveals it through the prophetic ministry (Ps. 139:16, Jer. 29:11).

The prophetic ministry can therefore be defined as God revealing His plans or thoughts for a person, place, or situation by using a minister or servant.

When it is said that someone is prophetic, it means he or she ministers under divine inspiration from God through one or more of the prophetic gifts, which I will discuss later. One of the key questions when considering this book is, "Is this ministry still the will of God for this generation, or has He stopped talking to His people as He did in biblical times?"

Is God Still Speaking Prophetically?

This question is very important to consider for those who wish to walk in the prophetic way. The simple answer is yes, God is indeed still speaking prophetically, and He wants to talk to you and through you. God has and always will speak through the mouths of the prophets and prophetic believers when He wants to do something on the earth (Amos 3:7).

The Holy Spirit

In John 16:12, Jesus says there are still many things He has to say to us. He said this because He was going to place the Holy Spirit inside all of us who believe in Him. And it is through the Holy Spirit that Jesus communicates in our lives and in the lives of others. Jesus also said,

> When He, the Spirit of truth, has come, He will guide you into all truth; for He will not speak on His own authority, but *whatever He hears He will speak,* and *He will tell you things to come.* He will glorify Me, for *He will take of what is Mine and declare it to you.* (John 16:13–14, emphasis added)

The good news is that as a believer, you have the Holy Spirit within you, which means God can speak to you and through you at any time. First Corinthians 3:16 says, "Do you not know that you are the temple of God and that the Spirit of God dwells in you?"

As a result of this truth of the indwelling Holy Spirit, the conclusion then becomes that the prophetic ministry is for everyone. Therefore, *you do not have to be a prophet to be prophetic.* As long as you have the Holy Spirit, you qualify to hear from God. In the Old Testament, only a few people were qualified to hear from God. Those who heard from Him were particularly prophets. This is no longer the case for New Testament believers.

So whether you want to hear the voice of God for your own life or wish to minister to others, this book is for you. You will realize as you continue to read that *God wants to talk to you and through you.*

God has good plans for all of us. In Jeremiah 29:11, God says this concerning our lives: "'For I know the thoughts that I think toward you,' says the LORD, 'thoughts of peace and not of evil, to give you a future and a hope.'"

God wants to unfold this good plan in our lives and wants us to know about it. The only way we can ever know the wonderful plans and thoughts God has for us is to tap into the prophetic ministry.

The Five Steps

In part 2 of this book, I will discuss the five steps God has shown me that are key to prophesying and moving in the prophetic gifts. They are listed below but discussed in detail later in the book.

Step 1: Appreciate the biblical truth concerning the prophetic ministry.

Step 2: Desire the prophetic gifts for yourself.

Step 3: Open yourself to receive the prophetic message from God.

Step 4: Know how to release the prophetic message.

Step 5: Know when and if to release the prophetic message.

Reflection

The word *prophetic* can refer to all the ways in which God communicates in and through people.

Can you remember the five steps without looking? Give it a try.

- Do you believe God can speak to you and through you? If not, why?
- All believers are ministers in one way or another.
- The prophetic ministry can be defined as God revealing His plans or thoughts for a person, place, or situation by using a minister or servant.

Exercise

- Try to remember some of the prophets you have learned about and where God spoke through them. This may require you to look in the Bible.
- Try to remember a time when you believed God was speaking to you. Write it down.

Prayer

Father, I thank You that as I read this book You will fill me with revelation knowledge through the Holy Spirit in the prophetic ministry. Thank You for using these gifts for the benefit of Your plans in my life and for Your people. In Jesus' name. Amen.

CHAPTER 2

Prophetic Gifts and Their Purpose

What Are Spiritual Gifts?

Before we focus on the prophetic gifts, I would like to teach you a bit about spiritual gifts. Prophetic gifts are a portion of the spiritual gifts that are spoken about in the Bible.

Spiritual gifts come as a result of receiving Jesus Christ and His Holy Spirit and are available to all believers by faith. Let us look at 1 Corinthians 12:4–10, which identifies nine of the spiritual gifts.

> There are diversities of gifts, but the same Spirit. There are differences of ministries, but the same Lord … But the manifestation of the Spirit is given to each one for the profit of all, for to one is given the word of wisdom through the Spirit, to another the word of knowledge through the same Spirit, to another faith by the same Spirit, to another gifts of healing by the same Spirit, to another the working of miracles, to another prophecy, to another discerning of spirits, to another different kinds of tongues, to another the interpretation of tongues. (emphases added)

Spiritual gifts are those things God places in our spirits that enable us to serve Him when we are born again. As I mentioned, there are several spiritual gifts mentioned in the Bible (Rom, 12:6–8, 1 Cor. 12:8–10, Eph. 4:11). In fact, there are at least twenty-eight spiritual gifts identified in the Bible.[1] In this book, I focus on the prophetic gifts.

Prophetic Gifts

There are four main prophetic gifts:

- word of knowledge
- word of wisdom
- discerning of spirits
- prophecy

The first three gifts are commonly known as the *revelation gifts* because they are revealed, and prophecy is known as an *utterance gift* because it is uttered or spoken. In this book, I have termed all four of them *prophetic gifts* because they all are a means of communicating the heart and mind of God. (Remember our definition of the prophetic in the previous chapter.) Let us now look at what they mean.

Word of Knowledge: This refers to the Holy Spirit revealing past or present facts about a person, place, or situation that may include names, numbers, or any other information. This differs from human knowledge in that the information is unknown to the natural mind of the prophetic minister until God reveals it.

---

1   C. Peter Wagner, *Discover Your Spiritual Gifts*. Ventura, California U.S.A.: Regal Books, 2005.

Examples of Word of Knowledge in Operation

Example 1

In 2 Kings 5, after Elisha directed Naaman to receive healing by dipping himself in the Jordan River but refused to take any money or material from him, Elisha's servant, Gehazi, then went to Naaman and lied to him, saying he was sent by the prophet to receive money and other material possessions. God revealed to Elisha what was happening, and later, when Gehazi came back, Elisha said to him,

> Did not my heart go with you when the man turned back from his chariot to meet you? Is it time to receive money and to receive clothing, olive groves and vineyards, sheep and oxen male and female servants ...? (2 Kings 5:26)

Example 2

In John 4, the Bible relates an interesting story. Jesus is sitting next to a Samaritan woman at a well and begins to reveal to her the many husbands she has had throughout her life. Jesus also reveals her acts of adultery. He says to her, "You have well said, 'I have no husband,' for you have had five husbands and the one whom you now have is not your husband; in that you spoke truly" (John 4:17–18).

Word of Wisdom: This refers to the Holy Spirit giving guidance and direction for solving a particular problem, a God-inspired way to solve problems. This differs from human wisdom in that the wisdom comes directly from God, not our own natural wisdom. God usually reveals a situation through the *word of knowledge* and then gives the solution through a *word of wisdom.* These two gifts usually operate together.

Examples of Word of Wisdom in Operation

Example 1

In Genesis 41, Joseph interpreted a dream Pharaoh had concerning two types of cows that represented a future time Egypt would have of prosperity and famine.

To solve the problem of the coming famine, Joseph received a *word of wisdom* that they should collect one-fifth of the produce of the land of Egypt in the seven plentiful years and store up the grain, that Egypt would not perish during the famine (Gen. 41:34–36).

Examples of Word of Knowledge and Word of Wisdom in Operation

Example 1

God may reveal to you that a believer does not have direction for his ministry because he spends all his prayer time reading other ministers' material (*word of knowledge*). The *word of wisdom* may be that God wants to have him or her spend time alone with only Him and the Bible for the next year, and from that time, direction and revelation for his or her ministry will come.

Example 2

A believer comes to you and cannot understand why she is so scared to start a business even though she knows she has a calling into business. The Holy Spirit may then reveal that the person has neglected her time in the Bible (*word of knowledge, because it is a past and present fact*). A *word of wisdom* may be if God inspires you to tell the person: "If you can spend at least thirty minutes daily for a few days reading the victories God won for the Israelites in the book of Joshua, the fear will go and the faith in you will arise."

What we can notice from the above examples is that the *word of knowledge* is the *what*, while the *word of wisdom* is the *how* and the *when*. Remember that when God reveals a problem to you using the word of knowledge, always press in for a word of wisdom for the solution so the person is fully ministered to. This is because *God reveals a problem to redeem the situation.*

Discerning of Spirits: This is when the Holy Spirit reveals the type of spirits operating in a particular person, place, or situation. These may be angels, demons, or the Holy Spirit. This is not being perceptive or being a "good judge of character" because that comes from the natural mind while this gift is revealed in the spiritual mind.

Examples of Discerning of Spirits in Operation

Example 1

In 2 Kings 6, the Bible records that an army had gathered around Elisha and his servant. Elisha, sensing the angelic presence, said to his servant,

"Do not fear, for those who are with us are more than those who are with them." And Elisha prayed, and said, "Lord, I pray, open his eyes that he may see." Then the Lord opened the eyes of the young man, and he saw. And behold, the mountain was full of horses and chariots of fire all around Elisha. (2 Kin. 6:16-17)

Example 2

In Acts 14:7–10, while preaching, Paul discerned that a crippled man was moving in faith to be healed. The Bible records,

> And in Lystra a certain man without strength in his feet was sitting, a cripple from his mother's womb, who had never walked. This man heard Paul speaking. Paul, observing him intently and seeing that he had faith to be healed, said with a loud voice, "Stand up straight on your feet!" And he leaped and walked.

Example 3

A believer may come to you who complains of constant headaches and blackouts and asks you to pray for healing. Just as you are about to pray, the Holy Spirit may reveal to you that the cause of the headaches is not a medical sickness but instead a demonic spirit that needs to be bound and cast out.

Prophecy: This refers to when the Holy Spirit communicates the heart and mind of God for a particular person, place, or situation. Prophecy can be in the past, present, or future. When a prophecy is given, it can carry within it some or all of the other three revelation gifts. See example three below.

Examples of Prophecy in Operation

Example 1

Isaiah, prophesying the ministry of Jesus, said,

> There shall come forth a Rod from the stem of
> Jesse and a Branch shall grow out of his roots.
> The Spirit of the Lord shall rest upon Him, The
> Spirit of wisdom and understanding, The Spirit
> of counsel and might, The Spirit of Knowledge
> and of the fear of the Lord. (Isa. 11:1–2)

Example 2

Joel prophesying of the army of the Lord that shall be
raised in these days said,

> So I will restore to you the years that the locust
> has eaten, the crawling locust, the consuming
> locust, and the chewing locust, My great army
> which I sent among you. (Joel 2:25)

Example 3

In the middle of a prayer meeting, the Lord may inspire
you to give the following prophecy:

> I perceive that there are many gathered here
> with a healing and counselling ministry (*word of
> knowledge*). The Lord says, "Continue to gather in
> my name, for soon I shall bring many broken and
> sick to be restored and healed in this meeting"
> (*prophecy*). The Lord says as we have been desiring

to see many saved in this area, this will happen when we intercede daily for this place and go through a forty-day fast (*word of wisdom*). I sense that angels are standing and waiting to do warfare on the demonic spirits of false religion that are operating in this place (*discerning of spirits*).

Other Prophetic Gifts and Expressions

There are other prophetic gifts through which the Lord can express Himself through a person, place, or situation. They include:

Prophetic Song: This is when the Holy Spirit inspires a believer with words to a song to sing or to write down. The song may be sung in public or in a private time with God. This type of gift may also be in the form of *prophetic psalms,* or *poems* to God.

Prophetic Dance: This is when the Holy Spirit inspires the believer to move his or her body in a certain way.

Prophetic Praise and Worship: This is when the believer is inspired to praise and worship God in a specific way as led by the Holy Spirit for God to accomplish something.

Prophetic Prayer: This is when believers are inspired to pray for certain things that God has revealed to them either for their own lives or for others. When the prayer is for others then it becomes *prophetic intercession*. Many times *prophetic prayer and prophetic praise and worship result in prophetic spiritual warfare.* This where God uses the prayers and praise of believers to bring down demonic strongholds. All believers who have a call for intercession should press into these gifts and function in them for effective and accurate prayer. As much as we must all intercede, there are others who have this burden from God more than others.

Prophetic Acts: This is when believers perform certain actions in the physical to represent what they want to see happen in the spiritual realm. For example, this could be using your hands to pull down your property from heaven or rolling on the floor to represent rolling over the nations for God. This may be led by the Holy Spirit or activated by the believer.

Biblical Command to Move in the Prophetic Ministry

The Bible says we as believers must *"pursue love,* and *desire spiritual gifts but especially that you may prophesy"* (1 Cor. 14:1). This says to me that God has given us all a command to prophesy and therefore wants all of us to prophesy. God in this Scripture is not *suggesting* that we prophesy; He is *instructing* us to desire this precious gift.

God takes the prophetic ministry very seriously and so should we. Whatever is important to Him should be important to us. We must also understand that *God would not want us to desire something if He did not want to give it to us.* One translation tells us to "covet" the gift of prophesy. That word is *zeloo* in the Greek, which means to *enthusiastically pursue after.* In other words, don't stop until you get it. It is the only gift in the Bible we are told to covet.

Let us now look at why God would give us such a command by looking at the reasons for the prophetic ministry.

Reasons for the Prophetic Ministry

Before we learn *how* to be prophetic, we must learn *why* we need to be prophetic. God is serious and passionate about the prophetic ministry, and I believe now more than ever before, He wants His people to move in this ministry as we get ready for His return.

To fully understand the reason for the prophetic ministry, we must first understand that God only operates according to His Word. According to Psalm 138:2, God has put His Word even above Himself.

This means God cannot decide one day to change His plans and His Word for our lives. His Word governs even Him, *but* God needs His Word to be released on the earth to accomplish His plans (Jer. 1:12).

This is true not only for the prophecies written in the Bible but also for the prophetic word through the mouth of a believer. So let us start prophesying to labour with the Holy Spirit to build the kingdom of God on the earth.

Three Main Reasons for the Prophetic

According to the Bible, "...he who prophesies speaks *edification*, and *exhortation* and *comfort* to men" (1 Cor. 14:3, emphases added).

Let us now look to see what the above three words mean to us.

Edify: This word in the Greek is *oikodome*, which means to *build, erect, or put stones into place*. The prophetic has the power to build the spiritual and physical world. God told the prophet Jeremiah that the prophetic words can actually build or tear down a nation:

> Then the Lord put forth His hand and touched my mouth, and the Lord said to me: "Behold, I have put *my words in your mouth*. See, I have this day set you over the nations and over the kingdoms, to *root out* and to **pull down**, To

destroy and to throw down, To build and to plant." (Jer.
1:9–10, emphasis added)

For example if you prophesy to a person and say: *"God wants you to
preach His Word,"* this has the effect of working in a person's mind and in
the person's spirit and when mixed with faith it releases the angels and
the Holy Spirit to move in the spiritual realm and to bring the message
into manifestation.

Exhort: This word in the Greek is *paraklesis,* which means to offer
"comfort" or "consolation." It also has the meaning of "a calling near to
or a calling for a Divine purpose."[2]

We all often face discouraging times, but when you release a prophetic
word, it has the power to lift up that person to continue trusting in God
for the fulfilment of his or her calling and for God's divine purpose in his
or her life.

For example, a believer may be tired of serving God, and wants to
quit the ministry. Then the Lord reveals to you a vision where you see this
person as an umbrella and many believers are under him, symbolizing
his influence and spiritual covering over them. And in the vision the
umbrella keeps getting larger, signifying increase in his or her ministry.

This type of prophetic message will help keep the person in ministry
serving the Lord by boosting his confidence because he has seen the
impact of his ministry over others, with the promise of increase from the
Lord in the future.

Comfort: This word in the Greek is *paramuthia,* which also means to
console or comfort but also has the meaning of to *"speak closely to someone."*
When this type of message is released to a person, it can comfort him or

---

2   Jonathan David, *Moving in the Gifts of Revelation & Prophecy.* Johor, Malaysia
Destiny Heights, 1993. Pg. 26,27.

her and will allow the Holy Spirit to minister to that person in a special and intimate way.

For example a man's wife has left him for another man because of lack of money, and she wants to divorce him. He has tried to win her heart, but she insists on divorce and eventually carries on with it despite his best intentions to keep the marriage. The Lord may then reveal to you in a dream or vision where you see the man smiling and happy with another woman in marriage, standing on a mountain of gold.

By interpretation the Lord says tell him, "I have prepared someone for him, and He will increase in wealth." This word will comfort or console the brother till he sees that day.

So we notice that the prophetic message in whatever way it comes must *edify*, *exhort*, and *console* or comfort. Therefore any prophetic message that contradicts this principle is not a true word from God.

Examples of prophecies that are false may be:

- "God wants you to have an affair."
- "God says you should stop tithing and pay your debts."
- "God wants you to remain sick, poor, or in sin."
- "I had a dream/vision that you are opening up a nightclub, and I saw you selling lots of alcohol and making money for the church."

The above examples are *clearly false* prophetic messages because they all involve *sin* and *disobedience* to the Word of God. But more specifically, these messages do not *edify*, *exhort*, or *console* in a scriptural manner. Even if a prophetic message comes to reveal a person's sin, the objective of the message is always to stop the sin and rebellion so God can build the believer's life again.

Below are some other reasons I have identified for prophetic messages.

The prophetic message allows God to perform His will on earth: It allows God to move through the Holy Spirit and His angels to perform His plans. By releasing the prophetic word, you are setting the course for the prayer "Your will be done on earth as it is in heaven" (Matt. 6:10). When put differently or in another way, it can be said that when releasing the prophetic word, you are joining as a kingdom builder with God.

It convinces unsaved people about the gospel of Jesus Christ: When you release a prophetic message to unsaved people, it becomes easier to get them saved. It makes you an effective and powerful witness of Jesus and the cross. Unbelievers often need the supernatural power of God to believe our message of the cross. Paul put it this way:

> But if all prophesy, and *an unbeliever* or an *uninformed person comes* in, he is *convinced* by all, he is *convicted* by all. *And thus the secrets of his heart are revealed*; and so, falling down on his face, *he will worship God and report that God is truly among you.* (1 Cor. 14:24–25, emphases added)

In Acts 1 Jesus told His disciples that the only way they were ever going to be effective witnesses of the cross was to operate with the Holy Spirit. This is because when the Holy Spirit came, He came with His gifts, which are the tools for effective witnessing.

> And being assembled together with them, He commanded them *not to depart from Jerusalem, but to wait for the Promise of the Father,* "which," He said, "you have heard from Me; … *But you shall receive power when the Holy Spirit has come upon you:* and you shall be witnesses to Me in Jerusalem, and in all Judea and Samaria, and to the end of the earth. (Acts 1:4–8, emphasis added)

It gives way for the use of other spiritual gifts to operate: A prophetic message presents a platform for other gifts to function in you and in the person receiving the message. *The Lord reveals to redeem.* He will not allow something to be revealed prophetically if He did not want to solve it. Let us look at some examples to appreciate what I mean by this.

Example 1

For example, the Lord may show you that a person is struggling with a pain in his or her body. When this is revealed, then the *gifts of healing* can rise up to solve that problem (1 Cor. 12:9).

Example 2

The Lord may reveal that a person is having a major financial challenge and needs a large sum of money. When this is revealed, it can give room for the *gift of faith* to rise up and provide for that need (1 Cor. 12:9). You can learn more about the different spiritual gifts in books by C. Peter Wagner and Kenneth Hagin recommended at the end of this book.

It counters the false spiritual voices that are present today: The truth is that many people out there are looking for answers to life's problems. However, a lot of them, including believers, are looking to lying spirits, like horoscopes, psychics, and the occult.

The prophetic voice is the only true voice that can change people's lives. Jesus said, "The words I speak are truth and they are life" (John. 6:31). One prophetic message can remove bondages of sin, sickness, curses, depression, suicide, addictions, poverty, etc., forever. As believers, let us activate this supernatural gift and provide solutions to the hurt, lost, and broken.

Reflection

- There are four main prophetic gifts.
- God always reveals to redeem.
- One prophetic word can remove bondages and change a person's life forever.

Exercise

- Write down and describe the four main prophetic gifts, and look for examples of them in the Bible.
- Ask the Lord to give you a prophetic song for you to sing to Him. You can even combine it with a prophetic dance.
- What does it mean to say, "God reveals to redeem"?
- Have you ever looked for your future through horoscopes, psychics, or any other way than God? If *yes*, then repent before the Lord and pray the second prayer below. If *no*, then continue to stay away from this demonic activity.

Prayer 1

Father, thank You for opening the eyes of my understanding to the many reasons for the prophetic ministry and causing me to take it seriously so I can serve the church of the Lord Jesus Christ and see many lives changed. Father, I invite You to express Yourself through me in prophetic song and dance now in Jesus' name. Amen. (The key is to open your mouth and let Him fill it with words and the melody and allow your body to move.)

Prayer 2

Father, for all the ways I have searched for my destiny or life through any method outside the Bible (*mention these ways*), I confess it as sin and ask

You to forgive me now in Jesus' name. Lord Jesus, I declare You to be the only one who knows and controls my future, so Lord, I loose myself from any demonic ties in my life as a result of psychics, horoscopes, or any method of fortune telling. Lord, I claim and receive my deliverance now in Your name, Jesus. Amen.

CHAPTER 3

How Does God Speak?
Language of the Prophetic Ministry

This chapter covers the manner in which God speaks and how to recognize His voice. As you study this section, most of you will realize God has been speaking to you already for a long time. Some frequently asked questions by believers include:

- How does God speak?
- How can I hear the voice of God?
- How do I know when God is speaking to me or through me?

These are the questions I seek to answer in this chapter, and to do this, we have to learn the many different ways in which God communicates to His people.

Different Ways God in Which Speaks

Listed below are some ways I have identified in which God speaks according to the Bible. It is important to note that *God speaks to us in several ways, and we should never limit Him* to speak to us in a certain way. We must open our spirits to receive any way in which He wants to communicate with us.

(1) His Word (*logos and rhema*)

(2) Dreams and visions

(3) Trances

(4) Pictures or images

(5) Still, small voice

(6) Loud, audible voice

(7) Thoughts

(8) Impressions

(9) Lack of comfort or peace

(10) Physical signs

(11) Angels

(12) The prophet or prophetic minister

Let us have a closer look at the meaning of the above.

His Word (Logos and Rhema): The logos is the written Word or the Bible. This is the most reliable way God speaks, and all other ways must be tested against the Bible. The rhema means a revealed word. It is when the Holy Spirit allows a Scripture to come alive and become personal to you. In Luke 4:18–19 we can see as one example in the Scriptures where Jesus discovered His ministry through a rhema word in Isaiah 61:1–2.

> The Spirit of the Lord is upon Me, Because He has anointed Me To preach the gospel to the poor He has sent Me to heal the broken hearted, To proclaim liberty to the captives And recovery of sight to the blind, To set at liberty those who are oppressed; To proclaim the acceptable year of the Lord.

Dreams and Visions: This is when the Holy Spirit speaks to a believer through pictures and words when the believer is *asleep* in a dream or *awake* in a vision. An example of a dream from the Holy Spirit is found in Genesis 37:5–8 where God revealed the future of Joseph to him. It says,

> Now Joseph had a dream, and he told it to his brothers; and they hated him even more. So he said to them, "Please hear this dream which I dreamed: There we were, binding sheaves In the field Then behold, my sheaf arose and also stood upright; and indeed your sheaves stood all around and bowed down to my sheaf."

In Acts 7:55–56 we can see that just before Stephen was killed by the Jews, he saw a vision.

> But he, being full of the Holy Spirit, gazed into heaven and saw the glory of God, and Jesus standing at the right hand of God, And said. "Look! I see the heavens opened and the Son of Man standing at the right hand of God!"

Trance: This is a deeper and more intense form of a vision. In a trance, your physical senses often become unoperational, and your spirit becomes open to receive a message from God in pictures and words. In Acts 10:10–16, the apostle Peter had this encounter:

> The next day, as they went on their journey and drew near the city, Peter went up on the housetop to pray, about the sixth hour. Then he became very hungry and wanted to eat; but while they made ready, he fell into a trance and saw heaven opened and an object like a great sheet bound at the four corners, descending to him and let down to the earth. (Acts 10:9–11)

Pictures or Images: This can be described as when an image or picture flashes in your spirit once or several times. An image or a picture is another form of a vision but may not be as detailed as a vision. Jeremiah the prophet had this encounter in Jeremiah 1:11:

> Moreover the word of the Lord came to me, saying, "Jeremiah, what do you see?" And I said "I see a branch of an almond tree."

Still, small voice: This is God speaking within a believer heard with the *spiritual ear*. The voice may sound like your own voice, but the words are His. In 1 Kings 19:11–13 Elijah had this experience:

> Then He (God) said, "Go out, and stand on the mountain before the Lord." And behold, the Lord passed by, and a great and strong wind tore into the mountains and broke the rocks in pieces before the Lord, but the Lord was not in the wind; and after the wind an earthquake, but the Lord was not in the earthquake; and after the earthquake a fire, but the Lord was not in the fire; and *after the fire a still small voice.* So it was, when *Elijah heard it,* that he wrapped his face in his mantle and went out and stood in the entrance of the cave. Suddenly a voice came to him. (emphases added)

Loud, audible voice: This is God's voice heard from the outside with your physical ears. An example of this is found in the apostle Peter's experience in Matthew 17:5–6.

> While he (Peter) was still speaking, behold, a bright cloud overshadowed them; and suddenly *a voice came out of the cloud,* saying, "This is My beloved Son, in whom

I am well pleased. Hear Him!" And *when the disciples heard it,* they fell on their faces and were greatly afraid. (emphases added)

Thoughts: This can be described as when constant thoughts, plans, or ideas are given by the Holy Spirit. The Bible encourages us to think like God, and often God will give us His thoughts. Philippians 2:5 says: "Let this mind be in you that was also in Christ Jesus." Further in 1 Corinthians 2:16 the Bible says, "We have the mind of Christ ..." Many times when God speaks, He will use your thoughts.

Impressions: This is sometimes called an *unction.* It is a strong feeling deep within you to do or say something from the Holy Spirit. In the book of Jeremiah, the prophet had this kind of experience when he resisted prophesying as the Lord impressed him to do. God made the decision not to release the prophetic words unbearable for him. He describes it this way:

> Then I said, "I will not make mention of Him, nor speak anymore in His name. But *His word was in my heart like a burning fire* shut up in my bones; I was weary of holding it back, and I could not." (Jer. 20:9, emphasis added)

Another illustration is found in Acts 18:5 where the Bible says Paul "was compelled by the Spirit" and testified to the Jews that Jesus is the Christ (emphasis added).

Lack of Comfort or Peace: This is when the Holy Spirit causes a lack of comfort or peace within a believer as an indication that He disapproves of something. However, a sense of peace or comfort about a decision or action usually means one has His release to go ahead with that decision or action. In Acts 15:28, Paul says,

For *it seemed good to the Holy Spirit, and to us*, to lay upon you no greater burden than these necessary things. (emphasis added)

Lack of comfort or peace is also used by the Holy Spirit to convict us of sins (John 16:5–14). This conviction is usually a *gentle reminder* of the sin to lead us to repentance. Condemnation is different because it is *loud* and brings with it *negative thoughts and emotions*. Condemnation comes from our unrenewed minds and from the Devil, not from the Holy Spirit.

Physical signs: God may use physical signs or things to express Himself. We can see an example of this in Acts 21, where Agabus the prophet warned the apostle Paul with a physical sign by binding a belt around himself to symbolize or foretell the danger that awaited Paul in his journey to Jerusalem.

And as we stayed many days, a certain prophet named Agabus came down from Judea. When he had come to us, *he took Paul's belt, bound his own hands and feet*, and said, Thus says the Holy Spirit, So shall the Jews at Jerusalem bind the man who owns this belt, and deliver him into the hands of the Gentiles. (Acts 21:10–11 emphasis added)

Also in the book of Hosea, God instructed the prophet to marry a harlot to symbolize His marriage to the unfaithful Israelites. God said to him:

Go, take yourself a wife of harlotry and the children of harlotry, for the land has committed great harlotry by departing from the Lord'. So he went and took Gomer the daughter of Diblaim, and she conceived and bore him a son. (Hos. 1:2–3)

Angels: God may release angelic beings to give a message to you for yourself or for somebody else. We can see that God caused John to have angelic visitations when he wrote the book of Revelation. An extract of this is taken from Revelation 17:1, where the Bible records:

> Then one of the seven *angels* who had the seven bowls *came and talked with me, saying to me,* "Come, I will show you the judgment of the great harlot who sits on many waters." (emphases added)

The prophet Daniel is also an example of someone who received prophetic messages through angels. Daniel was fasting and waiting on God when he saw an angel. He describes it as follows:

> Now on the twenty-fourth day of the first month, as I was by the side of the great river, that is, the Tigris, I lifted my eyes and looked, and behold, a certain man clothed in linen, whose waist was girded with gold of Uphaz! His body was like beryl, his face like the appearance of lightning, his eyes like torches of fire, his arms and feet like burnished bronze in color, and the sound of his words like the voice of a multitude. (Dan. 10:4–6)

The Prophet or Prophetic Minister: In this instance God speaks through those who have the office of the prophet or function in the prophetic ministry. There are several examples in the Bible of this type of communication. The prophet Elisha prophesied that the Shunnamite woman would have a son.

> Then he said, "About this time next year you shall embrace a son." And she said, "No, my lord, man of God, do not lie to your maidservant!" But the woman conceived, and

bore a son when the appointed time had come, of which Elisha had told her. (2 Kings 4:16–17)

David prophesied about the way Goliath would die.

> This day the Lord will deliver you into my hand, and I will strike you and take your head from you. And this day I will give the carcasses of the camp of the Philistines to the birds of the air and the wild beasts of the earth, that all the earth may know that there is a God in Israel. (1 Sam. 17:46)

Reflection

- The Bible is the most reliable way God speaks, and all other ways must be tested against the Bible.
- God speaks to us in several ways, and we should never limit Him to speak in a certain way.

Exercise

- Name at least seven different ways in which God speaks that you have learned in this chapter.
- Try to look back and remember any ways in which God has spoken to you in the past, and write them down. There may be several, so dig deep.
- Which ways do you desire God to speak to you the most in the future? Write them down, and then ask Him.

Prayer

Father, I pray in the name of Jesus that You would open my eyes to all the different ways You can speak to me. I pray I will not limit You in the ways You want to talk to me. Father, my desire is that You would in the future speak to me through *(mention the ways you desire the most)*. Amen.

PART 2

The Five Steps to Get You Prophesying

CHAPTER 4

Step 1: Appreciate the Biblical Truth Concerning the Prophetic Ministry

The Bible is the starting point for every teaching, and all teachings must fall within it. If you believe like me that the Bible is the absolute truth and the ultimate God-inspired Word according 2 Timothy 3:16, then by the end of this chapter, you will be convinced about the truth, which is that *God wants to place and activate the prophetic ministry in you and through you.*

This chapter is important because unless the scriptural truth about this ministry is revealed to you, it will have been a waste of time for you to pick up this book. The Bible says in Psalm 119:130 that the entrance of the Word of God brings light. This chapter and this step are therefore the starting point and the foundation for the prophetic ministry functioning in your life.

As we will learn, the prophetic ministry is active throughout the Bible. Revelation 19:10 says: "The testimony of Jesus is the spirit of prophecy." This means Jesus used the *four prophetic gifts* we have already learned about. Jesus Himself needed to be empowered by the Holy Spirit, just as we need to today (Acts 1:8, 10:38). The Bible says that as He is so are we in this world (1 John 4:17).

The truth is that all of us must be prophetic and not only pastors or leaders. God makes a promise in Joel 2:28–29, which says,

And it shall come to pass afterward that I will *pour out My Spirit on all flesh*; your sons and your daughters shall prophesy, your old men shall dream dreams, your young men shall see visions. And also on My menservants and on My maidservants I will pour out My Spirit in those days. (emphasis added)

This verse is telling us that God will release the prophetic ministry in the last days like never before. These are the last days, and we are the generation the Lord is pouring out the abundance of His Spirit on. One of the reasons for this is so we can move in the prophetic ministry. This Scripture does not give the prophetic gifts to leaders but to *all* who will receive it by faith.

When God speaks of sons and daughters, young men and old men, it shows us that people of all ages, colour, sex, or race can move in this ministry. There is no discrimination with God (Rom. 2:11, Gal. 3:28). God Himself takes delight in speaking the end from the beginning. In Isaiah 46:9–11 God says,

Remember the former things of old, for I am God, and there is no other *declaring the end from the beginning*, and from ancient times things that are not yet done, saying, 'My counsel shall stand, And I will do all My pleasure calling a bird of prey from the east, the man who executes My counsel, from a far country. *Indeed I have spoken it; I will also bring it to pass* I have purposed it; I will also do it. (emphasis added)

God cannot declare the end from the beginning on the earth without a human vessel. Everything in the future that God desires to do needs a human vessel to first receive it and then to release it. Amos 3:7 says,

> Surely the Lord God does nothing, Unless He reveals His
> secret to His servants the prophets.

What is even more amazing is that God watches over His prophetic word to perform it. Jeremiah 1:11–12 says,

> Moreover the word of the Lord came to me saying,
> "Jeremiah, what do you see?" ... Then the Lord said to
> me, "You have seen well, for *I am ready (watching) to
> perform My word.* (emphasis added)

God is readily available to perform the prophetic message, but He needs you and me to release it into the natural, here on the earth. Isaiah 44:21–26 says,

> Thus says the Lord, your Redeemer, and He who formed
> you from the womb "I am the Lord who makes all things"
> Who stretches out the heavens all alone ... *Who confirms
> the word of His servant,* and performs the counsel of His
> messengers. (emphasis added)

First Corinthians 14:5 says,

> I wish you all spoke with tongues, *but even more that you
> prophesied*; for he who prophesies is greater than he who
> speaks with tongues. (emphasis added)

Here Paul is saying that as much as the gift of tongues is important, the greater gift is to prophesy. This is because of the benefits it has to people who are both saved and unsaved.

In Isaiah 45:11, God probes us to inquire from Him. He says, "Ask

Me of things to come concerning my sons." This sounds to me like God really wants to reveal some of His secrets to us.

Reflection

- God wants to place and activate the prophetic ministry in you and through you.
- All believers must be prophetic and not only pastors and leaders.

Exercise

- If you are not yet convinced that the prophetic ministry is for everyone, then please go through the Scriptures again and pray the prayer below until it becomes truth to you. Judge yourself on a scale of one to ten, with one being not convinced and ten being fully convinced. Meditate on this chapter until you have reached at least six out of ten.

Prayer

Holy Spirit, You are the Spirit of truth, so I pray in Jesus' name that You give me revelation knowledge of the prophetic ministry and open the eyes of my understanding so I may see my position in the prophetic ministry according to the Word of God. Amen.

CHAPTER 5

Step 2: Desire the Prophetic Gifts

Now that you have received revelation about the truth of this ministry, the next step is to develop and increase the level of hunger or desire you have for it.

We have already seen in 1 Corinthians 14:1 that the Bible tells us this gift is important enough to be coveted or to be strongly pursued or desired. *The truth is that God gives us according to our level of hunger.* Matthew 5:6 says, "Blessed are those who hunger and thirst for righteousness for they will be filled." James 4:2 says we do not have because we do not ask.

We see according to these two Scriptures that *God encourages us to hunger and to ask Him for spiritual things.* In Luke 11:5–13, Jesus gives a parable about the persistence of prayer, especially for the Holy Spirit, and promises to give us nothing less.

The parable in Luke 11:5–13 is very important for encouraging you to develop this desire, so let's look at what it says,

> And He said to them, "Which of you shall have a friend, and go to him at midnight and say to him, 'Friend, lend me three loaves; 'for a friend of mine has come to me on his journey, and I have nothing to set before him'; and he will answer from within and say, 'Do not trouble me; the door is now shut, and my children are with me in bed; I cannot rise and give to you'? I say to you, though he will

not rise and give him because he is his friend, yet because of his persistence he will rise and give him as many as he needs 'so I say to you, ask, and it will be given to you; seek, and you will find, and knock and it will be opened to you. *For every one who asks receives, and he who seeks finds, and to him who knocks it will be opened* If a son asks for bread from any father among you, will he give him a stone? Or if he asks for a fish, will he give him a serpent instead of a fish? Or if he asks for an egg, will he offer him a scorpion? If you then, being evil, know how to give good gifts to your children *how much more will your heavenly Father give the Holy Spirit to those who ask Him!"* (emphasis added)

In the Scriptures we note that Jesus took pleasure in those who pressed in by faith into what He had to offer. The same applies even today because Jesus is the same yesterday, today, and forever (Heb. 13:8). He still longs for His children to press into Him for what He has. This is why He told us to be persistent and not give up. The reality of a hunger for spiritual things is that it produces faith within us. God is pleased by our faith, and that is when He rewards us (Heb. 11:6).

Psalm 63 is one of my favourite psalms. It talks about desiring the things of God. Read it and allow it to encourage you to hunger for the prophetic ministry. Psalm 63:1–2 says,

O God, You are my God; early will I seek You; my soul thirsts for You; my flesh longs for You in a dry and thirsty land where there is no water. So I have looked for You in the sanctuary, to see Your power and Your glory.

Reflection

- God gives us according to our level of hunger and desire.
- God encourages us to hunger and to ask and believe Him for spiritual things.

Exercise

- Read Psalm 63:1–2 again and reflect upon your own life to see if you have ever desired to see the power and the glory of God in this way.

Prayer

Father, according to Your Word, You respond when I hunger for the things of Your kingdom. I ask that You stir up a hunger and a passion within me that will move You to pour out a measure of the prophetic ministry into my life by the power of the Holy Spirit. In Jesus' name, amen.

CHAPTER 6

Step 3: Learn to Open Yourself to Receive the Prophetic Message from God

Let us reflect on what we have learned so far. By now you should have appreciated the scriptural truth about the prophetic ministry, and you should have developed or increased in your desire to operate in this ministry.

Your next step is to open your spirit to receive from God, and one of the keys to being open for the Holy Spirit to deliver a message is to wait on Him. This may come immediately or may take time. *However, the best way to receive from God is to spend time alone with Him,* where you can have uninterrupted fellowship. This time allows the "many voices" of the world to be drowned by the beauty of His voice as His presence consumes you.

Opening your spirit to receive from God is an act of both *faith* and *patience.* The Bible says in Hebrews 6:12, "We inherit the promises of God through faith and patience." The prophetic ministry is a promise and will require these principles to grow and develop.

The following are some activities you can do to open your spirit to receive a prophetic message from the Holy Spirit.

(1) Keep a notebook and pen ready next to you, and call it something like "Holy Spirit Speaks" as an act of faith and expectation.

(2) Write down thoughts, impressions, and pictures that keep coming to you in prayer or at any other time during the day. This is called journaling.

(3) After a time of private praise, worship, and prayer, ask the Lord to show you something concerning a place, person, or situation, and then wait for Him to talk to you in the ways I have already mentioned. Stay silent in His presence for a few moments.

Below are some areas you can ask the Lord to reveal to you concerning a person. (Taken from Dr. Jonathan David's book *Moving in the Gifts of Prophecy and Revelation*.)

Area of need: This is all about identifying the need the person has. For example, the Lord can reveal to you in a *trance* that a person is struggling to pay her bills or has challenges in her life and needs the Lord's strength.

Area of commendation: This is the area where you can compliment the person in his walk in life or with God. For example the Lord can show you in a *dream* that the person is spending time with Him and this pleases Him. Or the Lord can reveal that a certain person has good leadership skills.

Area of gifting or calling: This is the area of God-given gifts and talents. For example, the Lord can reveal a *vision* where a person is standing in a boardroom full of businesspeople giving a presentation, signifying that she is going to succeed in the marketplace. Or an *angel* of the Lord can tell you He has called a person to evangelize and heal the sick.

Area of oppression or stagnation: This area can include bondages, weakness, or sin in person's life. For example, while you are reading Isaiah 61, verses 1 and 2 keep appearing in your spirit together with a certain person, and the Holy Spirit gives you peace that the word is a *rhema* for him.

Area of provision for the person: This is an area of what the Lord has in store for a person in spiritual and physical needs. For example, the Lord may impress on you to give a person a key as a *physical sign* of a new door of opportunity opening in her life.

Area of future plans: This is an area of what the Lord has in store for the future for the person. *Note* this is what can be termed a "future prophecy" and should be exercised with caution or *not at all* when you are beginning in the prophetic ministry. For example, the Lord can speak to you in a *still, small voice* and say, "This person is My chosen servant, a king I will use to make millions in money for My church, and in three months, I will cause him to sign a contract to mining rights."

These examples are given to help open you to the different ways in which God speaks and the types of messages He may give. *Do not limit God to speak a particular thing or to speak in a particular way,* but open your spirit and stretch your faith to receive any revelation from any of the different ways God speaks. *As you tune into the prophetic flow regularly, you will be able to discern the way in which God speaks to you the most.* Soon you will establish the confidence of knowing when God is speaking and when it is merely your imagination.

Be Aware of the Spirit of Fear

The spirit of fear will try to come in different ways to hinder the prophetic flow in your life. You must learn to identify this spirit and destroy it in the name of Jesus.

For example, some of you may be filled with fear that you will receive a message from an evil spirit. Or you may fear you are now engaging in a new age practice. These fears are justified by many because they believe they are being cautious. As much as being cautious is important, it must never hinder you from moving in new levels with God because of fear. You must learn to trust God that *if you ask for a fish, He will not give you a serpent* according to Luke 6:5–13. Remember, all messages you receive must be tested against the principles discussed in chapter 1 anyway. So then make a decision today to reject any spirit of fear and receive *the spirit of power, love and a sound mind* (1 Tim. 2:7). *Fear has never progressed any ministry but will slow you down.*

You may also fear you will get a revelation, interpretation, or application wrong. The truth is that this might indeed happen, but you must understand that our Lord makes room for our mistakes. Sometimes these mistakes cause you to grow in wisdom and maturity in the gifts of the Spirit. Just ensure that you follow all the guidelines highlighted in this book to minimize any mistakes, and should you make a mistake, then continue to press into the time when you will not be making mistakes. That time will surely come. Our God's grace is always available.

Reflection

- The best way to receive prophetic messages from God is to spend time alone with Him.
- Do not limit God to speak a particular thing or to speak in a particular way.

- As you tune into the prophetic flow regularly, you will be able to discern the way God speaks to you the most.
- God wants to place and activate the prophetic ministry in you and through you.
- Reject any spirit of fear, and receive the spirit of power, love, and a sound mind (1 Tim. 2:7). Fear has never progressed any ministry, but it will slow you down.

Exercise

- Once a week ask the Lord for a prophetic message concerning someone in an area you have learned about in this chapter. Write down the message you have received, and then approach the person and ask if the message is relevant to his or her life. You can start with close friends or family members to build your confidence and accuracy.
- Make a habit of writing down messages you believe are from the Lord concerning your life.

Prayer:

Father, I ask and thank You that as I wait on You, I will receive messages from You concerning (*tell the Lord which area you want to receive a message in and for whom*). Here I am, Lord, open to receive from You in Jesus' name. (*Continue to thank God until the message is given and becomes clear*).

CHAPTER 7

Step 4: Learn and Know How to Release the Prophetic Word

This topic covers the type of words you use when you give a prophetic message. The "*how*" part of releasing the prophetic word is very important, because of the following reasons:

(1) Your words may *hurt another person*, depending on the approach you take. For example if God reveals to you that a brother has a drinking problem, a harsh approach may be, "You're a drunkard, and you are going to hell," but a gentle approach may be, "Brother, I just want you to know I am trusting God for you to overcome the drinking problem."

(2) It may *cast a bad reputation on the prophetic ministry*, causing people to lose faith in a true move of God. Many people are afraid when they hear the word *prophet* or *prophetic* because of many mistakes people have made and are still making. I believe God is restoring faith in this move of the Holy Spirit through me and other prophetic ministers. I would urge all believers to receive and teach the balanced and scriptural prophetic ministry and not reject it altogether.

(3) It may *cause people to discredit you* and hinder further prophetic messages. If you were sincere and people talk about your mistake, just admit your mistake and God will make your gift grow until

it cannot be hidden any longer. The key is never to give up and to always keep trying.

(4) It may *cause hurt to you and discouragement* from receiving and giving further prophetic messages. Again here it is important to note that if you were sincere and cautious and got a message wrong, then keep pressing into this ministry until you perfect it. I have often missed God before, but now my accuracy has increased because I did not allow discouragement to defeat the hunger I had inside of me.

Making Sense of a Prophetic Message

Prophetic messages may not always come in a manner in which our natural minds may understand (1 Cor. 2:14). At times we may struggle to make sense of the message, and until we know what it means, we must not apply our own interpretation of how it should apply to other people or in our own lives. At times a message may come that you will only understand after a long period of time. You must be prepared to wait if necessary. Your responsibility is to press in for the meaning of the message by faith with the help of Spirit of revelation knowledge living on the very inside of you, and trust Him to reveal the meaning in His time.

If the message is for someone else and you cannot make sense of it, then you may just tell the person what you saw or heard without giving meaning to it. The Holy Spirit will work with that person to make the message clear to him or her. *You do not always have to know the meaning of the message, especially if it is for someone else.* Daniel and other prophets gave prophetic revelations about the future that are only making sense now.

If the message is for you, then I encourage you to write it down and break it up into different portions for it to make sense.

Below are some principles to help you make sense of prophetic messages.

Revelation, Interpretation, and Application

These are three important principles to remember when releasing the prophetic message. I remember them by calling them *RIA,* which stands for *Revelation, Interpretation,* and *Application.*

- **Revelation:** This is the actual message you receive, in the different ways it may come that were mentioned earlier.
- **Interpretation:** This is the meaning given to the message. It may require you to do some research because the meaning of the message may depend on different things, like numbers, colours, and places that are symbolic and mean different things in the Bible. A good book or website can assist you to give meaning to the message.
- **Application:** This covers how the message should be applied in reality. It is useless to have a message and a meaning and not know how to apply it in your life.

Example of RIA in Operation

Revelation

You have a dream, and in that dream you are standing in a *dry desert place*, and you *pick up your dusty Bible* on the floor. Immediately when you *open it, you are transported to a green place with fresh water.*

Interpretation

Dry desert place: You are in a tough place surrounded by discouraging and tough situations.

Pick up your dusty Bible: You are picking it up because it was not in your hand all along, and it is dusty because you have not been reading it.

Open it and you are transported to a green place with fresh water: Opening and reading the Word will result in you being taken to a place of rest and prosperity.

(Remember to break it up into portions if it has a lot of detail in it, like I have done in this example.)

Application

God recognizes the dry situation, and He is revealing to you that it is not permanent. It is present because you have neglected the Word. Begin to read the Word, and the dry place will be replaced quickly by the prosperity and rest of God.

Other Important Principles to Remember on How to Release the Prophetic Message

Prophetic messages must be according to our grace and faith. The Bible tells us that we must exercise our gifts according to the proportion of our faith. Romans 12:6 says,

Having then gifts *differing according to the grace that is given to us*, let us use them; if prophecy, let us prophesy in proportion to our faith. (emphasis added)

By grace I mean the degree or level of enablement or anointing of the gift operating in our lives. Like many things God gives us, there is a time when it begins and a time when it grows. It is important to assess yourself continually on the level of grace operating in your life, before speaking with certainty on what you believe God is saying or wants to reveal through you.

Below are some examples of words to avoid and words to use when giving the prophetic word.

Words to Avoid	Words to use Instead
"Thus says the Lord ..."	"I believe the Lord is telling me to tell you ..."
"The Lord has showed me ..."	"I believe I saw in my spirit ..."
"In twenty-one days the Lord shall ..."	"I trust the Lord will do this soon for you."
"You have a pain in your right leg, on your hip."	"Do you have a pain in your body or in any of your legs ...?"
God is going to bless you with a 5 series silver BMW, 2012 model.	"I believe the Lord is going to bless you with a car, I believe I heard/saw a BMW." (The less the detail the better as you start, to avoid many inaccuracies.)

I encourage you to press into the highest dimension of revelation knowledge by faith. If you desire to one day accurately call out people's names, phone numbers, destinies, etc., then go for it. However, remember to begin by executing the little you have faithfully and in the proportion of faith and the depth of revelation God has given to you. The less information you give the better when you are in the beginning stages.

This principle is also true when you are asked to interpret or apply a prophecy or prophetic message. Do not rush to do so, and if you are not certain, you can simply say, "I am waiting on God to clarify it or to speak to me." This is a careful way to avoid giving reckless and unconfirmed prophetic messages. It is also a statement of faith because it says, "I know God uses me prophetically, so I will wait." This is different from saying, "I don't know."

(1) *Prophetic messages must be given in the fruit of love.* All spiritual gifts should be motivated by the fruit of love. *Love for both God and His people is the main reason behind the prophetic ministry and all other ministries.* These gifts are not a toy or a badge but a tool to build His kingdom. We must always strive to serve others with these gifts in the attitude of love.

This fruit of love becomes highly important when dealing with the *motives* in our hearts for wanting to prophesy. Accurate prophetic ministry can bring a lot of attention to you. However, the motive behind it should never be to receive recognition for you but always for God.

The fruit of love is also important when we *feel hurt or rejected* by people. The question is, *will we still want to give the message from God for His people?* Pain through criticism will always come from people, but this should never taint our love for God's people and desire to see them moving in the destiny He has for them through the prophetic word. This is precisely the purpose of prophecy. It is for God to fulfil His plans.

Let us look at some scripture that speak about the fruit of love and its importance. First Corinthians 13:2 says,

> And though I have the gift of prophecy, and understanding all mysteries and all knowledge; and though I have all faith, so that I could remove mountains, *but have not love, I am nothing.* (emphasis added)

First Corinthians 13:13 says,

> And now abide faith, hope, love, these three; *but the greatest of these is love.* (emphasis added)

First Corinthians 13:8 says,

> Love never fails. But whether there are prophecies, they will fail.

Always remember, love is the reason the Father sent His Son to die for us (John 3:16), and love is the reason we have received these gifts. *It is because of His grace and love that you will move in the prophetic ministry and not because you deserve it* (2 Tim. 1:9).

Reflection

- The Bible tells us that we must exercise our gifts according to the proportion of our faith and the grace (*enablement or anointing*) on our lives.
- The less information you provide, the better when beginning.
- Love for both God and His people is the main reason behind the prophetic ministry and all other ministries.
- You do not always have to know the meaning of the prophetic message, especially if it is for someone else.
- It is because of grace that you will move in the prophetic ministry and not because you deserve it.

Exercise

- Try to remember a prophecy, dream, or vision you received before or that somebody else received and write it down. Then apply the RIA principle as you have learned it in this chapter.

Prayer

Father, I thank You that my understanding for the prophetic ministry grows in interpretation and application of all revelations You show to me. Father, I ask that the fruit of love will always be the driving force behind my prophetic ministry and that the Holy Spirit will enable me to prophesy according to the faith and grace upon my life. In Jesus' name, amen.

CHAPTER 8

Step 5: Learn and Know When and If to Release the Prophetic Word

This is the principle of timing. It deals with when the prophetic message should be released. The first thing to note is that the prophetic message is not to be released when it is convenient but when the atmosphere permits it, in love and sensitivity to those around you. Below are some factors to consider when releasing the prophetic word.

A *Private* Word or a *Public* Word

At times the message you receive may be of a sensitive nature and cannot be shared where there are people because it may embarrass the person receiving the message. It may also be too explicit if children are present.

For example, the Lord may reveal to you that a couple is having trouble with sexual intimacy. You should not announce this in front of the church or where people are present.

The Lord may also reveal to you that a person in the church is bitter and jealous against a certain person. This type of message too cannot be spoken in public because it may cause more harm than good if spoken.

In these instances mentioned, it is best to call the person aside in private and convey the message in a sensitive and compassionate way, keeping in mind Galatians 6:1.

> If a man is overtaken in any trespass, you who are spiritual restore such a one in a *spirit of gentleness*, considering yourself lest you also be tempted. (emphasis added)

In John 4 Jesus spoke privately to the woman at the well concerning issues of adultery in her life. As a result she was touched, and this opened up doors for the whole village to receive the gospel. Always strive to figure out, through the help of the Holy Spirit, the nature and the content of the message, and be mindful of those around you.

A *Now* Word or a *Future* Word

The Lord may give you a word to be released immediately, or at times, the Lord may ask you to hold on to that word until a future date. For example, the Lord may reveal to you that He has impressed upon a person to release a financial blessing into your life. It may seem like you are greedy if you release that word before the person gives it to you, but after the person blesses you, you can say something like, "The Lord showed me that He laid it on your heart. Thank you for your obedience."

A *Secret* Word or a *Sharing* Word

At times the Lord may reveal to you something but may ask you to keep it to yourself. This principle applies both for you and for someone else. In Genesis 37 we can see that Joseph told his brothers a secret word that came to him through dreams. This lack of wisdom on *when* and *if* to release the prophetic word caused him a great deal of trouble. *This shows us that a prophetic word released before its time can cause more harm than good.* He should have kept the word between him and God and revealed it only when God gave him the go-ahead.

A secret word for your life may be who God has revealed for you to marry, the type of ministry He will give you in the future, etc.

If the message is for another person, the Lord may ask you to intercede for that person or just be a friend to him or her.

When you receive a message, ask the Holy Spirit whether the word is a secret between you and Him or whether you can share the word with someone.

Reflection

- When releasing a prophetic word, always consider: whether it is a private word or a public word; whether it is a now word or a future word; and whether it is a secret word or a sharing word.
- A prophetic word released before its time can cause more harm than good.

Exercise

- If you have ever given a prophetic word, consider it and whether it was released at the right time.
- Ask the Lord to give you a secret word for your life, and then write it down. Make this a habit.

Prayer

Father, I thank You that the Spirit of wisdom governs me whenever I want to release a prophetic word. Thank You, Holy Spirit, for teaching me to be mindful of Your timing and those around me. In Jesus' name, amen.

CHAPTER 9

Other Keys for Growing in Effective Prophetic Ministry

In this chapter I discuss important principles that are not already covered that govern the prophetic ministry according to the Bible. When these principles are followed, they will result in a greater depth and frequency in receiving and releasing prophetic messages. If you're reading this book, it is because you wish to have a deeper and more frequent communication with God. These are the principles worth knowing.

Judging and confirming prophetic messages: Allow your prophetic messages to be judged for accuracy and scriptural truth by other prophetic ministers. This principle is based on the following Scriptures:

> Do not despise prophecies. *Test all things;* hold fast what is good. (1 Thess. 5:20–21 emphasis added)

> Beloved *do not believe every spirit, but test the spirits,* whether they are of God. *(1 John 4:11, emphasis added)*

> Let two or three prophets speak, and *let the others judge.* *(1 Cor. 14:29 emphasis added)*

59

> By the mouth of two or three witnesses every word shall
> be established. (2 Cor. 13:1)

In a practical way, first this would involve going to people who are more mature than you are in the prophetic ministry. Second, it would mean encouraging the people you prophesy to, to approach mature prophetic ministers for confirmation. Third, it would involve encouraging people to record or write down the prophetic words you give. This can also prevent misunderstandings about what was and was not said.

Some or all of these processes may be hard on the flesh, but allowing your prophetic messages to be judged or confirmed regularly will produce accountability, humility, maturity, and accuracy. It will prevent you from error, which so many fall into, because they do not allow for spiritual checks and balances. May this not happen with you.

Prayer and time with spent God: Fellowship with God is the reason God created us. I am almost certain nothing means more to God than when we desire to spend time with Him and make the time available for Him. Therefore I would urge you to spend time in prayer, especially praying in the Spirit daily. (I recommend for at least one hour daily). *The more you pray in tongues and spend time with God, the more sensitive you become to His voice and leading.* In James 4:8, God says draw near to Him and He will draw near to you. To know the hidden things of God, you must learn to be close and intimate with Him through prayer.

I believe the reason the Holy Spirit used Paul to write more than half of the New Testament is because he spent a lot of time with God. He says these key words:

> I thank my God *I speak with tongues more than you all.* (1
> Cor. 14:18 emphasis added)

I once heard James W. Goll, a prophetic minister, say the reason he is able to produce so many prophetic materials is because he spends at least two hours a day praying in the Spirit.[3] Apostle Maldanado in his book *How to Walk in the Supernatural Power of God* attributes a strong prayer life as being key to walking the power of God. He puts it this way: "Hours spent with God and turn into minutes spent with man."[4]

Spending time *reading the Scriptures* will also activate your prophetic ministry. The Bible, especially the Old Testament, is full of prophets we can learn from. *Praise and worship* is another powerful tool to enter the spiritual realm and to receive from God.

Regular use of the prophetic gifts: The more you put the prophetic ministry to use, the more it will grow in you. Make it a habit to ask and receive prophetic messages for your life and for the lives of others, and minister it to them. I heard Apostle Maldonado say there is a principle in the kingdom that states *you will lose what you do not use.*[5] I believe very much in this principle. The more you empty yourself for His service, the more God will fill you. God cannot fill those who are full or choose not to empty themselves out.

Jesus illustrated this principle in the parable of the talents in Matthew 25:29 when He said,

> For to everyone who has, *more will be given,* and he will have abundance; but *from him who does not have, even what he has will be taken away.* (emphasis added)

Also in Luke 16:10 the Bible says:

---

3   James Goll's material can be found at www.ministrytothenations.org

4   Guillermore Maldonado, *How to Walk in the Supernatural Power of God* Whitaker House, New Kensington, PA. 202.

5   CD series entitled *Leaders Walking in the Supernatural* (Disc 2) (www.elreyjesu.org).

He *who is faithful in what is least is faithful also in much;*
and he who is unjust in what is least is unjust in much.
(emphasis added)

Fruit of the Spirit or lifestyle of the believer: Although we receive all gifts by grace, our character and the fruit of the Spirit in and through us are important to God. Read Galatians 5:19–25.

Your lifestyle includes seeking a holy life before God and staying away from the things that would grieve Him. According to the Bible, God "has saved us and called us with a *holy calling,* not according to our works, but according to His own purpose and grace which was given to us in Christ Jesus before time began" (2 Tim. 1:9).

Pursuing holiness and the development of the fruit of the Spirit will ensure that the gifting in you grows and God will bring you before many to reveal those gifts He has put in you. *Remember, it is not the gifts that God looks at the most but our fruit and lifestyle. God can give you gifts in a day but cannot build your character in a day or without your cooperation.* Let us remember that, because "He who called you is holy, you also be holy in all your conduct" (1 Pet. 1:15).

It is also important to pay attention to what we watch with our *physical eyes* and what we listen to with our *physical ears* because this can have an effect on our *spiritual eyes* and *ears.* It can taint the prophetic ministry from operating in our lives. The Bible in Proverbs 4:23 says we must guard our hearts with all diligence.

Prophetic Material: Expose yourself to prophetic material. This includes books, CDs, video clips, DVDs, etc. I encourage you to read books of prophetic ministers you admire. This will cause your faith to be challenged and will also cause you to receive an impartation of the anointing they carry. Impartation of the prophetic ministry may also come through watching them on television or listening to their messages.

I also encourage you to sow your finances and prayers into the ministries that inspire you and those God leads you to. To sow money or materials is not to buy the gift, but instead, God uses your gift as a point of contact to partake of the grace that is in their lives (2 Kings 4:–18, Matt. 10:41, Gal. 6:6–9; Phil. 4:16–18).

Let prophetic materials challenge you to hunger and strive for deeper levels of revelation from God concerning your life and the lives of others. If God did it for them then believe He can do it for you.

Public or corporate prophecy: Last but not least, learn to participate in public or corporate prophecy. The apostle Paul encourages this type of prophecy in 1 Corinthians 14:23–31. This type of prophecy occurs when you are moved by the Holy Spirit to give a word or message within a group of believers or at your local church. The following principles are important when exercising this type of prophetic flow.

(1) Always *wait for an opportune moment* so you do not interrupt the service. If necessary, approach one of your leaders or your pastor for permission. If the pastor or leader insists you tell him or her what the message is first, then do it. Even if the leader insists that he or she will announce the prophetic message, you should allow it. The message is more important than the person who gives it.

(2) Try to *avoid too much detail* in the message if you are just beginning, and avoid words like "thus saith the Lord," as already discussed in previous chapters.

(3) Learn as much as possible *not be critical of others* when they try to move in this ministry, especially when they make mistakes. With the same measure you judge you will be judged (Matt. 7:1–2).

(4) You *do not have to receive the message in the service* but can receive it in your prayer closet or at your own time. During one of the prophetic workshops I held at our local church where I activate people to move in the prophetic gifts, a prophet in training came to me a bit frustrated and said something like, "I never receive

any messages in the service like the other people, as much as I try. But when I am praying, I receive a lot of visions concerning some of the people here today." I then explained to him that it did not matter when the messages came and that he could release the message in our prophetic class. He was quite relieved to hear this. God in His sovereign will chooses to speak to us in whatever way He wants and when He wants. We cannot determine when He speaks to us.

(5) Give your messages in a *fruit of love and sensitivity*. Always be mindful that love is the motivation for all prophetic messages and sensitive information should be shared in private.

Conclusion

In conclusion, over the years I have seen the Holy Spirit gently and patiently grow the prophetic ministry within me. I deeply appreciate Him for never allowing me to give up, always increasing the dimension I move in, and making me the prophet I am today. *I am not there yet, but I am not where I was.* Yes I am still learning and still growing, and I believe this process will never end, for we know in part and we prophesy in part (1 Cor. 13:9). However I always press toward the higher calling.

That's the wonderful thing about walking with God; you can always look forward to increase, new levels, and big surprises. He made me leave a well-earning law practice to write this book to you, so I know He wants to give you these gifts and this ministry. I am limited in the wisdom I can impart to you in this book because of space and time, but I know the Holy Spirit will guide you into deeper and higher realms of the prophetic ministry as you follow these principles. In my personal experience, these are some of the prophetic ministers who have inspired my prophetic growth: Bill Hamon[6], Maposa Mufaro,[7] Ubert Angel,[8] TB Joshua, Manasseh Jordan,[9] and Benny Hinn.[10] I encourage you to search for video clips where they are moving in the prophetic ministry and watch them.

6   www.christianinternational.com.

7   www.manifestsons.co.za.

8   www.spiritembassy.com.

9   www.prophetmanasseh.com.

10   www.bennyhinn.org.

PART 3

A Word to Pastors and Leaders

CHAPTER 10

A Word to Pastors and Leaders

Dear pastors and leaders, I pray this book will spark a passion for the prophetic ministry in your lives and in your members. I believe God wants all His people and not only pastors and leaders to move in the prophetic, and the reason I included this section is to encourage you to expose your members to this type of ministry.

The truth is that God has begun the restoration of the fivefold ministry and with it the gifts that accompany these offices. God has been impressing it upon many pioneering apostles and prophets around the world that every believer must rise to his or her full potential in Christ. The Holy Spirit is raising all types of movements to demonstrate His kingdom through all believers.

The *apostolic and prophetic movement* has given birth to all kinds of different movements, such as the *saints movement, the manifest sons of God movement,* the *kings and priests movement,* the *glory movement,* etc. All of them are rising up with one message: we are all the representation of Christ on earth by the power of the Holy Spirit. The difference between the movements is just that some emphasize certain Scriptural truths more than others.

I urge all pastors and leaders to seek and get the revelation of the apostolic and prophetic movement and to *equip, activate, and release your people to move in this ministry.* When you do this, you are fulfilling the mandate of Christ, which is the equipping of the believers for the work of the ministry, for the building of the body of Christ (Eph. 4:11–13).

Therefore do not resist this move of the Spirit by being bound to the way things used to be done. This is religious, and it is the old wine. The new wine is being poured out, and revelation knowledge is coming forth like never before to all believers, showing them they can walk in the supernatural power of God and in the gifts of the Holy Spirit. If you resist this move of the Spirit and your members receive it, they will move in a higher realm of revelation than you do and become more relevant to the kingdom of God.

I may understand your potential fears that believers who operate in giftings often start to think they are better and more anointed and often start being rebellious. The truth, however, is that the apostolic and prophetic movement is restoring order to the church. Everyone will fit into their place, and all gifts and callings will operate in an attitude of submission for the *common good and benefit of all* (1 Cor. 12:7). This will happen while believers maintain respect for authority and leadership. According to Joel 2:7–8, everyone will march in their own ranks in these last days.

While you focus on building His kingdom by building His people, He will deal with the rest. God will deal with pride and rebellion in any form.

I believe the call of God in this season is for all pastors to be apostolic and prophetic. This means all pastors and leaders must either press into these offices if they feel a call or press into the gifts that move with these offices and train their members to do the same.

Simply put, in our church services every time we gather, these signs and more should be present: *word of knowledge, word of wisdom, discerning of spirits, healing the sick, casting out devils, miracles, signs and wonders.* See extracts from my book *The Apostolic and Prophetic Dictionary* for more clarity on these subjects.

The days of thinking about our local churches above His kingdom are over. You build His kingdom by activating and teaching spiritual gifts, and He will build your local church.

Below I refer you to *some* (not all) pioneers I believe God is using to bring this present-day move of the Holy Spirit—not only through the signs but also through their teachings. I would urge you to get some of their material.

- The apostolic movement and prophetic movement: Dr. Bill Hamon, Dr. Jonathan David, C. Peter Wagner, John Eckhardt
- Manifest sons of God movement: Maposa Mufaro.
- Glory and supernatural movement: Guillermo Maldonado, Joshua Mills, David Hertzog

May the Lord continue to increase your revelation knowledge until He comes again.

PART 4

Extracts from The Apostolic and Prophetic Dictionary

INTRODUCTION

This is a list of *some* of the words that have been taken out of my book *The Apostolic and Prophetic Dictionary*. The dictionary contains over *five hundred entries* and *over 430 present truths for the church today*. Only a few could be included in this book.

These extracts are also limited in the way they provide information. Once you read the format of the dictionary below, you will understand why. This format is also important for general understanding of the author's writing choice and style. It is important to obtain a copy of the dictionary.

Format as Taken from the Dictionary (PLEASE READ)

Some of the entries in the dictionary have the word "*See*" where the explanation should be given. This highlights that this term has been explained under the word or phrase mentioned after "*See*." For example:

Spiritual Gifts: See **Gifts of the Spirit**

Another handy feature is the insertion of "*See also,*" which appears at the end of some explanations. This is an indispensable connection of interrelated words or phrases that has been developed for the reader or researcher to obtain a richer meaning or deeper understanding of the words.

Words that appear **bolded** within the body of one explanation highlight that the word or phrase has been explained in the dictionary either on its own or within the body of another definition. It also highlights that the reader is encouraged to have a look at it.

The *Scriptures* explaining the phrase or words have been put either in the middle of the text (if directly relevant) or at the end (if generally relevant). It is the responsibility of the researcher to search out the Word for a deeper revelation and understanding of the word or phrase.

The *language choice* is British and South African English. Hence some spelling may differ from American English (e.g., honour-honour; favor-favour; checks-cheques).

It is worth noting that although some of the words in this dictionary apply in the *context* of the Bible and the secular world, I have chosen to confine them mainly within the context of the Word or kingdom of God.

It is also worth noting that I have used the *author's prerogative* and have written satan without a capital S. This is because I do not deem him worthy of such an honour.

WORDS AND PHRASES

A

Activation: This refers to the *act of triggering* or *stirring up* a gift or gifts within a believer so he or she can move in the grace of that gift or gifts. When activation is done, it releases the believer to move in that gift. Believers can be activated to: speak in **tongues**, prophesy, operate in gifts of **healing, deliverance, power to prosper, signs and wonders,** etc. **Spiritual gifts** are given by the Holy Spirit according to 1 Corinthians 12:4–11 and Romans 12:6–8, but they are activated by faith within the believer. Activation can come in several ways—for example, by attending a service or conference where the gift is practiced, during a time of **prayer** or **meditation**, by listening or reading certain material, or by receiving prayer or **laying on of hands** by a believer who moves in that gift (Rom. 1:11, 2 Tim. 1:6). *See* also **Impartation; Supernatural**

Anointing: This refers to the *ability or empowerment of the Holy Spirit to do what cannot be done by human effort.* The anointing comes to bring the manifestation of the Word of God in any area. The word anoint is *mashach* in Hebrew, which means to *pour, rub, smear,* or to *set aside* for God by using anointing oil. In the Bible, both people and objects were anointed, to consecrate or set them apart for God to use (Ex. 29:29, 30:25–29, 1 Sam. 16:13). Anointing oil is a symbol of the Holy Spirit and His enabling power and presence (1 Sam. 16:13, Acts 10:38). The anointing is therefore the *Holy Spirit rubbing Himself or pouring Himself on a believer to express or show Himself through the believer.* In a *physical sense* it can mean to pour, rub, or smear oil, but in a *spiritual sense,* it means to empower or come upon a believer. The anointing can be stored in physical objects and transferred, for example in and through clothing, handkerchiefs, water, oil, etc. (Acts 19:11–12, James 5:14-15). To be **anointed** means *to be set apart by God to be used in a certain way or to display or show a certain way the Holy Spirit operates.* **Christ** is *Hamashiach* in Hebrew, meaning the *Anointed One, with the anointing;* it is not the surname of the Lord.

Apostle: This is one of the fivefold ministries and a foundational office according to Ephesians 2:20, 4:11, and 1 Corinthians 12:28. This word is *apostolos* in the Greek, meaning *sent one* or *one who is sent.* It is an office entrusted by Jesus with the following: (1) to establish and correct doctrine; (2) to plant churches; (3) to oversee churches; (4) to pioneer new truths; (5) to impart and activate gifts and callings in others; (6) to network and form apostolic teams; and (7) to equip believers to perform their membership roles. The anointing, gifts, or grace that accompany apostles are usually special faith, healings, miracles, deliverance, and authority for opening spiritual realms for the kingdom to be established, etc. As the forerunner and pioneering office, apostles have the grace to bind strongholds for the kingdom of God to be built on the earth. False apostles are *unsent* by Jesus (Rev. 2:20). They do not pursue the objectives of the true Word of God; instead they are driven by false doctrine, selfish ambition, and sometimes satanic powers (1 Cor. 4:15, 2 Cor. 11:1–4, 28, Eph. 3:5). *See* also **Activation; Fatherhood; Fivefold Ministry; Impartation**

Apostle/prophet in the marketplace: This term may refer to two things. (1) It may be a believer who is an apostle or prophet in a priestly or a church setting where he or she has his or her main area of influence but also exerts some influence in the market place. (2) It also refers to a believer who functions in the anointing, gifts, or grace of an apostle or prophet but is called into the marketplace and not the church. The latter is the most common definition used today. Joseph, Daniel, and Esther in the Bible are examples of this type of believer. *See* also **Kings and Priests**

Apostolic and prophetic: This generally refers to any activity associated with the apostolic and prophetic gifts and principles. More specifically when it is said something or someone is apostolic, it means it or the person displays the functions, values, or characteristics that are in line with the office of the apostle. When it is said something or someone is prophetic, it means it or the person communicates the heart and mind of God somehow. This can be information from the past, present, or future, given meaning through the prophetic gifts. *See* also **Apostle; Apostolic believer / minister; Prophet; Prophetic believer / minister.**

Apostolic/ prophetic networks: These are different **apostolic and prophetic ministries** with common beliefs and visions who group themselves to support and pray for one another, share resources and material, and have oversight for accountability over each other. These networks often set up conventions and conferences together. Networks are established to have a larger and more effective impact in their regions and nations.

Apostolic and prophetic ministries: This refers to ministries that teach and practice the apostolic and prophetic principles and gifts. *See* also **Apostle; Apostolic gifts; Prophet; Prophetic gifts.**

Apostolic and prophetic order: This is the structure and order to be followed in the body of Christ according to 1 Corinthians 12:28. This structure emphasizes the need for mature and trained apostles and prophets to have the primary prophetic insight and apostolic oversight in all churches. *Prophetic insight* refers to the need of every local church to have either internal or external prophets to regularly provide *guidance* and *revelation* on the overall nature and state of the church. *Apostolic oversight* is the need for every local church to have *covering, oversight,* and *accountability* to apostles. It also has the meaning of believers being trained and released by apostles and prophets or apostolic and prophetic leaders. A local church, for example, cannot be started without God's timing and God's release. God communicates this timing and release to the believer, but it is confirmed and given oversight and insight by apostles and prophets as in the New Testament church. All churches and pastors need to follow this order because it promotes accountability and stability within the church. It also prevents leaders from being an authority unto themselves. The order can be achieved for example through partnering and spiritual mentoring. *See* also **Covering; Commissioning; Ordination**

Apostolic and prophetic pioneers: This term refers to apostles and prophets who establish new truths in the church. These pioneers often go against existing traditions and teachings within the church to establish or restore a new truth from the Holy Spirit and the Word. As a result, they often face much criticism and persecution. They often form foundations for new revelations and movements for all other believers to follow (1 Cor. 12:28, Eph. 2:20, 3:5). *See* also **Present truths; Restoration**

Apostolic and prophetic teams: This refers to ministries that teach and practice the apostolic and prophetic principles and gifts. *See* also **Apostle; Apostolic gifts; Prophet; Prophetic gifts**

Apostolic gifts: This refers to the gifts of the Holy Spirit that accompany the office of the **apostle** and **apostolic believers**. These may include: **deliverance, power, miracles, signs and wonders,** wisdom, **and training.**

Army of the Lord: This is a group of believers called from the church who form God's end-time army. This army has been prophesied to make more impact for God than any other generation before it according to Joel 2:2. Any believer can be a part of this army if he or she wants to. This is done by simply asking the Lord Jesus, who is the commander of the army, to enlist them. There is no limit to the number of believers in this army. This army will mainly show itself in the **kings and priests** model (Isa. 13:1–13, Jer. 51:20–23, Joel 2:1–11).

Authority: This word comes from the Greek word *exousia*. It means *delegated or conferred authority* or *authority that is given by one to another*. It can also mean *leave or permission to exercise dominion, jurisdiction, rulership, or leadership, or the influence of another with higher authority*. The authority of Jesus Christ is the highest authority in heaven, on earth, and beneath the earth (Phil. 2:8–11). Jesus, as the source of all authority, has given believers His authority. This means Jesus has given us the right to exert His rule on the earth and over satan. Authority gives believers the right to display the power or *dunamis* of God. Believers who are submitted under authority will display the greatest authority themselves. Just as Jesus submitted to the Father to receive all authority, even so believers must submit to Jesus and His **apostolic and prophetic order** to move in the highest manifestation of His authority (Matt. 28:18–20, Luke 10:19).

B

Believer: This refers to any person who has received the Lord Jesus Christ as his or her personal sacrifice for sin by saying and meaning the salvation prayer. Believers believe in Him as Lord, Saviour, and the only way to God and to heaven. A believer also relies on the Bible as the highest authority of truth on the earth (John 3:16–17, 14:6, 17:17, Rom. 10:9–100). *See* also **Salvation; Sinner's prayer**

C

Calling: This refers to the specific purpose for which a believer was born as given by God. It is often referred to as the **will of God**. God has called every believer for a specific and a unique calling, and it is obedience and faithfulness to this calling that will determine the rewards we receive in heaven from God (1 Cor. 3:12–15, Rev. 22:12). Every believer who desires to spend eternity with God must seek this calling with all of his or her heart and then depend on **grace** to accomplish it. The calling of God is accompanied by certain **gifts of the Holy Spirit,** which are tools to accomplish or fulfil the calling. The **general calling** or **general will of God** refers to the requirements God places on all believers. For example, all must gather in church services, all can marry only one other believer, all must sow financially, and so on. This general will is found in the written Word or *logos.* The **specific calling** or **specific will of God** refers to the exact details God wants to accomplish on earth using a believer. For example, the specific will of God will direct a person where to attend the service, which believer to marry, and where to sow financially. The specific will of God is found in the *rhema* or revealed word, which God gives to believers (Jer. 29:11–13, 2 Tim. 1:9). The calling can also relate to the **assignment** or **mandate** of God for a believer. This often refers to the specific task God has given a believer to accomplish for a specific time or **season**. Often many assignments will form part of the calling of God. The faithfulness we display in one assignment or mandate will result in a higher mandate or assignment (Acts 13:2, Rom. 11:29, Eph. 4:1, 2 Tim. 4:5). *See* also **Message; Ministry.**

Character: This refers to the *nature, traits, or qualities of a person that is seen in his or her actions, behaviour, and words.* The character of a believer is more important to God than the gifts or anointing upon his or her life. This is because *gifts are given* and *character is developed* within a person.

This can only be done when a believer yields to God over long periods of time. It is the character of a believer that will sustain his or her gifts and not the other way around. This is why the apostle Paul emphasized the need for proven characters in places of leadership and not gifts. God makes the man before the ministry is a term commonly used by a major apostolic and prophetic pioneer (Dr. Bill Hamon) to mean God places a lot more emphasis on the character and spiritual maturity of a believer before sending them out into wide public ministry. The bigger the impact of the ministry given by God, than the longer and more intense the character-building period will be according to Luke 12:48 (Matt. 7:20, Rom. 5:3–4, 1 Tim. 3:1–12, Titus 1:5–9). *See* also **Bishop; Deacon; Fruit of the Spirit; Spiritual Maturity.**

Church planting: This refers to the starting and establishment of new **local churches**. Church planting is usually done by **apostles** or **apostolic ministers**. Although not strictly necessary, there is usually a main or **parent** local church from which the others come. These new churches are also known as **branches**. Church planting involves **winning souls, training** them, and then placing them into positions where they can be used by God (Acts 14:21–23).

Commissioning: This refers to the sending out of believers by elders so they can accomplish their membership roles. This is usually a role of leadership. Being commissioned is a physical step with a spiritual purpose because with it comes the spiritual covering of the elders. In truth, Jesus has commissioned all believers to witness to the lost and demonstrate His power as given in Mark 16:15. This is known as the Great commission. However, commissioning of believers by elders is an orderly way by recognizing the gifts of a person and then releasing him or her to function in those gifts under oversight. It is usually done through prayer and by the laying on of hands of the elders. Being sent is different from being sent out. The former happens when an elder sends out believers, usually in teams to various places (for example streets, schools, villages, etc.) to witness and demonstrate the power of God (Num. 27:18–23, Matt. 28:18–20, Acts 13:2-4). *See* also **Apostolic and prophetic order; Membership ministry; Ordination; Prophetic presbytery.**

Conviction of the Holy Spirit: This refers to the gentle communication given by God within the believer to indicate He disapproves of certain actions or behaviour. The opposite of this voice is **condemnation,** which is a harsh, loud, and attacking voice of satan and his demons on the mind of a believer intended to cause guilt and shame. satan is an accuser, and his condemnation is always intended to point out failures and wrongs (Rev. 12:10). The conviction of God is always given to produce Godly sorrow, to lead the believer to **repentance**, and to restore them to the path of His perfect will (Rom. 2:4). Believers must learn to discern these two voices to avoid unnecessary thoughts of shame and guilt. Jesus did not come to condemn us but to bring His salvation and righteousness. God forgives all sins that are confessed (John 12:47, Rom. 8:1, 2 Cor. 5:7, 1 John 1:9). *See* also **Receptive to the Holy Spirit.**

Covering: This refers to the **spiritual covering** or protection over a person or ministry. Covering is usually provided for by ministries or ministers who have matured in ministry and who God has given **authority** in the **spiritual realm. Apostolic and prophetic covering** refers to the covering offered by **apostolic and prophetic ministries**. Covering can be obtained through submission under a ministry. It can also be obtained through service and obedience to the ministry or its leaders or sowing financially and through prayer from the covering ministry. Only ministries who are matured and confirmed by God can qualify to cover others. This is because God has tested and proven them. Covering is used for two main reasons: (1) to receive the gifts, grace, or anointing flowing from the head ministry, and (2) to receive protection from spiritual attacks. *See* also **Apostolic and prophetic order; Networking; Partnership.**

Creative miracles: This refers to when God supernaturally creates something that was not there before or was there but not functioning as it should. It can include human body parts, food, water, building material, money, etc. This type of miracle falls within the broader category of miracles as a gift of the Holy Spirit, and believers can trust God to move in it just as any other gift (Matt. 14:13–20, 15:30–39). *See* also **Gift of miracles.**

D

Demon/ devil consciousness: This refers to the mind-set of a believer that makes him or her more aware of the existence of demons and the devil and the potential danger they may cause, resulting in **fear**. This is different from **God/ Word consciousness,** which is the mind-set of a believer that makes him or her more aware of the existence of God and His promises and goodness, resulting in **faith**. Inasmuch as believers should have knowledge of **satan** or **demons**, this must never result in being fascinated or obsessed with the existence or study of demons to the point of thinking about them a majority of the time. However, it is also wrong to completely neglect the existence of devils because this will result in ignorance and unnecessary attacks from the enemy. The believer should be more God conscious because this will result in His presence, guidance, and protection (Phil. 4:8). *See* also **Meditation.**

Demonic/forbidden practices: This refers to activities and beliefs that are prohibited by God in His Word. Believers should stay away from these types of activities because they invite demonic spirits, which cause destruction and even death. These practices are **demonic doorways** or open doors that give satan a legal right to enter into the life of a person. Some of these practices include the following. (1) Human and animal sacrifices *and* (2) **divination,** which is the practice of inquiring into the future by using demonic powers. *This includes psychics, fortune-tellers, séances, mediums, soothsayers, diviners, spiritists,* etc., all use divination. These people often make use of *Ouija boards, astrology, horoscopes, numerology, tea leaves, palm* and *tarot card readings,* etc., to receive and give information. Any form of communication to God other than through the Bible and the Holy Spirit is a form of divination and is strictly forbidden by God (Lev. 19:26, 2 Kings 17:17–18, Acts 16:16–18). (3) **Magic/ witchcraft/ sorcery,** which is the manipulation of evil spirits to obtain a result. Witches (female magicians), wizards (male magicians), and sorcerers all use evil spirits to manipulate people and circumstances. Magic, witchcraft, and sorcery include practices like *casting spells, incantations, enchantments, use of potions* and *charms, familiar spirits* (demons invited by a person to guide them), etc. No magic is good magic. Both black and white magic are forbidden (Ex. 22:18, 1 Sam. 15:23, Isa. 47:9, Acts 8:9–11, Gal. 5:19–21). (4) this can include **new age** practices. (5) Generally all practices that place their faith in anything other than God are wrong. For example faith in *objects, herbs, "prophets," people, demons,* and *idols* are all forbidden by God. The **occult,** *satanism, omens, signs,* and all *false religions* and *belief systems* are also all forbidden by God (Deut. 18:10–12). Believers should not necessarily study all of these practices, but they should know *more or less* what they involve to avoid them and teach against them (2 Cor. 2:11). There are always demonic spirits behind every one of these practices. Once the spirit behind the activity is identified, it can then be bound or cast out by the believer. *See* also **Deliverance; False religion/beliefs; satan/demons.**

Deliverance: This is the *removal, binding,* or *casting out* of demonic spirits from operating in a person's body, soul, or spirit. It may also be called **exorcism**. Deliverance can be done through the **prayer** of another believer or by the oppressed believer using the Word of God. To be delivered and live demon free is a right of every believer, and nothing less should be accepted. The **deliverance ministry** is about bringing freedom to people who are controlled or oppressed by demonic spirits. Although all believers are called to live demon free and to exercise authority over demons, some believers have been given more grace by God than others to deliver people from demonic bondages and generational curses. These people are often referred to as **deliverance ministers**. Deliverance is done through the casting out of the devils or by binding their work and activity. Both of these are biblical ways of dealing with demons (Mark 16:17–18; Luke 10:19). *See* also **Demonic strongholds; Demonic/ forbidden practices; Generational curses; Spiritual warfare**

Demonic oppression: This refers to the operation of demonic activity in a person's life, causing different kinds of harassment. These can include mental attacks, illness, depression, lack, poverty, temptation, stagnation, etc. (John 10:10, Acts 5:16, 10:38, 1 Pet. 5:8). When a person becomes indwelt and controlled by demonic spirits, this is called demonic possession. At this stage, the demon dwells within the spirit and soul if the person is a nonbeliever and within the soul only if the person is a believer. This is because the spirit of a believer cannot be possessed because God dwells within it (1 Cor. 2:16, 6:19). Believers have the authority and the power to be delivered from demonic oppression and possession in Jesus' name. They also have the authority and power to cast out demons from others who are oppressed and possessed (Matt. 17:14–18, Mark 5:1–20, Acts 16:16–18). *See* also **Deliverance; satan / demons; Spiritual warfare.**

Demonstrations of the Holy Spirit: This refers to the display, manifestation, or exhibition of the power of God in the natural realm. It is also commonly called the demonstration of **power, kingdom demonstration, demonstrating the kingdom,** etc. Demonstrations of the Holy Spirit include but are not limited to the operations of the Holy

Spirit, gifts of the Holy Spirit, signs, wonders, and miracles. Every believer must be able to demonstrate God's kingdom in one way or another (Matt. 16:19, Mark 16:17–20, Luke 10:17, 19, 17:21, John 14:12, 1 Cor. 4:20). *See* also **Authority; Kingdom of God; Power**

Dimension: This refers to the *measure, level,* or *area* of **anointing**, gifts, or **grace** operating in the life of a believer. For example, moving in the apostolic dimension would mean displaying the signs or gifts of the apostle. *See* also **Glory to glory, Faith to Faith.**

Discerning of spirits: This refers to the gift of the Holy Spirit that reveals the type of spirits operating in a particular person, place, or situation. These may be angels, **demons,** or the Holy Spirit. This is not being perceptive or being a good judge of character because that comes from the natural mind. This gift instead is revealed in the spiritual mind by God (2 Kings 6:16–17, Acts 14:7–10). *See* also **Prophetic gifts.**

Dominion: This is the word *radah* in the Hebrew and it refers to the *rule* and *authority of royalty or a king.* It is used with the word *subdue* in Genesis 1:28, which is the word *kabash* in the Hebrew, which means to *enslave.* It also has the meaning of *defeating a military enemy.* Dominion was lost at the **fall of man** or Adam but was restored back to believers in **Christ.** Believers therefore can and must walk in this dominion. **Dominionists** are believers who practice and preach dominion as their central message. The **dominion movement** is the people around the world God is raising to preach and **activate** the message of dominion within believers. One of the central beliefs of dominion as a teaching is the reclaiming of the **seven mountain kingdoms** (Gen. 1:26–28, Ps. 8:6, Rom. 5:17, Col. 2:15, 1 John 3:8, 4:17, Luke 10:19). *See* also **Authority.**

Double-portion anointing: This refers to the type of empowerment or ability given by the Holy Spirit that multiplies, increases, or accelerates the anointing operating in a believer's life. The prophet Elisha asked for and received this enablement through the prophet Elijah (2 Kings 2:9–15). As a result of the double-portion anointing, he has more recorded miracles in the Bible. Any believer can ask and receive this multiplication of the Holy Spirit's empowerment. Even though the anointing multiplied by double in the case of Elisha, there is room for more than double in the case of the New Testament believer in Christ (1 Kings 17, 2 Kings 13). *See* also **Activation; Impartation; Mantle**

Dream: This refers to the communication given by God to a person through pictures (*stationary or moving*) and sometimes words while the person is asleep. *See* also **Vision; Trance** (Gen. 37:5–9, Matt. 1:18–25, Acts 2:17).

E

Edify/edification: This word (edify) in the Greek is *oikodome*, which means to *build, erect, or put stones into place*. Edification is one of the functions of a prophetic message according to 1 Corinthians 14:3. When a believer edifies another, they build up their spirit man and raise their faith levels by speaking words from God. Edification also has the ability to build God's purpose for a believer in the spirit realm because of its prophetic nature (Jer. 1:9–10). *See* also **Exhort / exhortation; Prophetic gifts**

Elijah spirit: This refers to an **anointing** that will enable believers to operate like Elijah with **authority** over kings, over evil spirits, in miracles, and in the **prophetic ministry**. The Elijah spirit is based on Scriptures like Malachi 4:5–6 and Mark 9:12–13, which speak about Elijah coming before Jesus. As John the Baptist was a type of Elijah before Jesus came on the earth, even so there will be a people God will raise as a type of

Elijah with the ability to operate like Elijah before the **second coming** of Jesus. The **Elijah company/type of prophets** refers to prophets who will operate as Elijah did. This teaching is amplified by the fact that Elijah left His mantle on the earth with Elisha, and even when Elisha died the mantle still produced miracles (2 Kings 2:9–13, 13:21).

End-time transfer of wealth: This refers to the *exchanging or redistribution of money, materials, land, resources, and influence from the control and hands of the unsaved into the hands of believers.* Popularly known as the wealth transfer, it may mean a *single transfer,* as in Exodus 3:19–22, and it can also refer to the *season* or a period prophesied and ordained by God in which this transfer will take place. The faith built around this concept centres on prophecies of Scripture. The church and believers are going to operate with dominion over the earth before the coming of Jesus, and this wealth will be needed for the largest harvest of souls or great harvest prophesied in these days (Deut. 6:10–12, Prov. 13:22, Eccles. 2:26, Isa. 60, Joel 2:23–27). *See* also **Power to prosper; Prosperity; Seven mountain kingdoms**.

End-time harvest: This speaks about the final move of the Holy Spirit to bring many to salvation in these last days. More souls will come than ever before to the saving power of Jesus as we wait for His return (Joel 3:14, Matt. 13:38–39). *See* also **Power evangelism/ witnessing ; Winning souls**

Evangelist: This is one of the fivefold offices mentioned in Ephesians 4:11. This word is translated from the Greek word *euaggelizo,* which directly means *a bringer of good news or good tidings.* Although all believers are called to evangelize or witness, evangelists are chosen and anointed by God especially for this reason. Evangelists have a unique ability to attract crowds and relate the gospel in such a manner that it convicts the hearts of the hearers, enabling many souls to be won to Jesus Christ.

The gifts, grace, or anointing that follow evangelists are usually special faith and miracles (Acts 21:8, 2 Tim. 4:5). *See* also **Power evangelism / witnessing: Winning souls**

Exhort/exhortation: This is one of the gifts of the Holy Spirit mentioned in Romans 12:8. It is the **grace** given to a believer to encourage others. This word *exhort* in the Greek is *paraklesis*, which means to offer *comfort* or *consolation*. Exhortation is one of the functions of a prophetic message according to 1 Corinthians 14:3. When believers exhort another, they boost the person's spirit to walk in the truth of God concerning his or her life. Comforting is one of the key functions of the Holy Spirit. The word *Comforter* referring to the Holy Spirit in John 14:16 is the Greek word *parakletos*, which literally means *someone who has been called to one's side to give aid and assistance*. Even though exhortation is a gift, all believers must exhort other believers. This is because exhortation encourages other believers to walk in that place where God wants them to be. Exhortation can give direction to a discouraged and directionless person. This is part of the commandment to **love** given to all of us by Jesus Christ according John 13:34–35 and His prayer in John 17 (Acts 15:31, Eph. 4:29, 1 Tim. 4:13, Heb. 3:13, 10:25). *See* also **Edify/edification.**

F

Faith confessions/decrees/declarations: All of these refer to speaking God's Word over a situation by faith. The Greek word for confession is *homolgeo*, which has the meaning of *saying the same thing God says and then agreeing with it*. It is also often called speaking the Word or speaking life. Believers must regularly confess God's word over the areas in their lives they want to see God change and affect. Just as God spoke things into existence (Gen. 1:1–25), even so believers have been empowered to do the same. The Bible empowers believers to speak things that do not exist as though they did so they will materialise (Prov. 18:21, Matt 12:37, 15:8, Rom. 4:17, 10:8, Heb. 4:12). *See* also **Faith; Prayer**

Faith: Faith is to *believe with eager expectation that what God has said concerning us is true and will happen for us.* Faith is a necessary ingredient to receiving answered prayers and for manifesting any spiritual gifts. The lack or absence of faith is unbelief. The source of faith is God's Word. The term *faith to faith* refers to the increase in the faith level that operates within a believer (Rom. 1:17). Faith is able to grow and increase as well as decrease. God calls every believer to ascend into new levels of faith in His Word. There are two main kinds of faith. The first is general faith, which refers to the faith we all receive when we become born again. It comes as a seed and grows according to the level of revelation we allow ourselves to receive from the Word of God. Faith can be placed both on the *rhema* and *logos*. It is therefore possible to have faith in the fulfilment of personal prophecies, visions, dreams, etc. The second kind is special/supernatural faith. This refers to the *quickening or the enhancing of a believer's level of faith for God to do a speedy work.* Special faith comes directly from God (1 Cor. 12:9). God operates where there is faith, so He does sometimes increase the level of faith in a believer to accomplish something for or through him or her. Special faith is usually accompanied by miracles. The opposite of faith is *fear and unbelief* (Matt. 13:58, Mark 11:22–24, Heb. 11:1, 6). *See* also **Faith confessions/decrees/declarations; Fear; Meditation; Supernatural boldness**

Fatherhood: This refers to mainly two aspects. The first aspect is the revelation of the Father of our Lord Jesus Christ being *accepted* and *appropriated* by believers to walk in the fullness as His sons and daughters. This relates to the *identity* of believers as sons and daughters of a loving Father. Believers must move beyond the revelation of salvation only and enter into the benefits of walking as sons and daughters of their Father. God is more than Saviour and King; He is also our Father and our Daddy

(John 20:17, Rom. 8:15, 2 Cor. 6:18, Gal. 3:26, 1 John 3:1). The second aspect speaks about the type of leaders God is raising in these days over His people. These leaders invest their lives as fathers would in their own children. This type of leadership style is called fathering. True apostles and prophets will bring about this selfless approach to leadership. Fathers in the faith (can also include mothers) refers to a man or woman God has used in the past and present who has become a mentor and a role model for others to follow (1 Cor. 4:14–15, 11:1). *See* also **Sons of God; Spiritual parents; Spiritual mentoring**.

Fear: *Webster's Dictionary* defines fear as "*a feeling of anxiety and agitation produced by the presence or nearness of danger, evil, pain,*" etc.[11] This is the opposite of faith. Fear should not be tolerated by believers because of the following reasons: (1) It is forbidden by God. The Bible mentions the phrases *fear not* and *do not fear* at least one hundred times (Deut. 31:6, Josh. 1:9). (2) God is restricted to release His promises where fear is present. This is because only faith pleases God (Matt. 14:26–31, Luke 8:49–55, Heb. 11:6). (3) Believers have nothing to fear because God is on their side, and nothing can defeat or override the Word of God (Ps. 23:4, Isa. 43:1–2, 54:17, Rom. 8:38–39). (4) Fear can allow demonic doorways, and permit satan and his demons to operate in a believer's life. This is because fear is from the devil. Fear is not a *mental force*; it is a *spiritual force* (2 Tim. 1:7). God is able to deliver believers from all fears when they are taken to Him in faith (Ps. 34:4, 1 Pet. 5:7). *See* also **Deliverance; Demonic oppression**

Fear of the Lord/God: Fear and trembling are two attributes the Bible encourages believers to have according to Philippians 2:12. These actually mean believers are to reverence and respect God more than

---

11   *Webster's New World College Dictionary*, Wiley Publishing, Inc., Cleveland, Ohio. 2010.

being terrified or afraid of Him. This is godly fear and reverence (Heb. 12:28). Believers must live with the fear of God. *Webster's Dictionary* defines fear as *"a feeling of anxiety and agitation produced by the presence or nearness of danger, evil, pain,"* etc[12]., but this fear of God does not involve an uneasy feeling of punishment or danger. Instead it is a love from within us to value and hold God in the high regard He deserves. Fearing God and loving Him are therefore one and the same thing. This fear is the only fear believers are allowed to have because it is not demonic in nature but comes from the Holy Spirit (Prov. 1:7, Isa. 11:1–2, Heb. 12:28–29). *See* also **Holiness; Repentance**

Fivefold ministry: This refers to the gifts or positions given to the church by Jesus Christ. The fivefold ministry is an extension of the ministry of Jesus. This ministry consists of the apostle, prophet, evangelist, pastor, and teacher according to Ephesians 4:11. They can sometimes be called fivefold ministers, offices, or positions. These ministries were given by Jesus when He ascended into heaven. Therefore, they are also called the ascension gifts. *Not every believer is called into these offices.* These offices *cannot* be imparted from one believer to another because they are given directly by Jesus from before birth. They have the function of equipping believers to work in their membership ministries to build the **body of Christ**. This function includes removing the divisions among believers by bringing unity and by establishing scriptural truths and doctrines and by exposing what is false (Eph. 4:12–16). *See* also **Kings and priests; Seven mountain kingdoms**

Fruit of the Spirit: This refers to the attributes or character of the Holy Spirit or God seen or evidenced through a believer. The word *fruit* means *that which is inward and comes out.* Fruit of the Spirit can also refer to the **character** of a believer. Generally the growth of a believer is seen in the fruit of the Spirit more than in the **gifts of the Holy Spirit**. The fruit

---

12   Ibid.

is listed in Galatians 5:22–23 as **love, joy, peace, patience, kindness, goodness, faithfulness, gentleness** (meekness), and **self-control** (self-discipline), but the fruit of the Spirit can also include holiness, righteousness, **praise and worship**, thanksgiving, etc. (1 Cor. 6:19, Col. 3:12–16, Phil. 4:4, Heb. 12:14). *See* also **Yielding to the Holy Spirit.**

G

Generational curses: This refers to curses and demonic operations that have been passed on from parents to their children, grandchildren, great-grandchildren, etc. These curses occur because of reasons such as sin, demonic or forbidden practices, involvement in the occult, and witchcraft. Generational curses do not leave simply because a person has received Jesus as Lord and Saviour. These curses can often be detected where there is a *trend, pattern, or similarities with generations from the same blood line*: a trend in *behaviour* (violence, anger, lust, abuse, etc.); a trend in *addictions* (drugs, alcohol, etc.); or a trend in *circumstances* (easy job losses, disfavour, premarital pregnancy, divorces, imprisonment, etc.). Put another way, generational curses can be identified where there are common problems or difficulties. This is one of the areas believers need to be free from after they have received Jesus as Lord. Breaking these curses is one of the reasons for which He came to the earth according to 1 John 3:8. Believers must also exercise their authority and pray over others who have generational curses (Ex. 34:7, Lam. 5:7, Gal. 3:13). *See* also **Deliverance; Demonic oppression; satan/demons**

Gifts of the Spirit: These are supernatural enablements given to believers by the Holy Spirit. They are also called **spiritual gifts.** There are at least twenty-eight spiritual gifts that can be identified in the Bible. Gifts of the Spirit are supernatural and have nothing to do with human strengths, capabilities, or talents. There are three broad categories of spiritual gifts mentioned in 1 Corinthians 12:8–10. (1) **Power gifts:** Working of **miracles, special faith, gifts of healing**. They are called power gifts because they demonstrate the power of the Holy Spirit. (2) **Utterance gifts: Tongues, prophecy, interpretation of tongues**. They are called utterance gifts because they uttered or spoken. (3) **Revelation gifts: Word of knowledge, word of wisdom**, and **discerning of spirits**. They are called revelation gifts because they come by revelation of the Holy Spirit. Gifts of the Holy Spirit that came with the Holy Spirit being sent to earth are called **descension gifts**, while ascension gifts refer to the **fivefold ministry**. Talents can often be confused with spiritual gifts, but they are not. This is because most talents proceed from the *natural* human being, whether the person is a believer in Jesus Christ or not. However, spiritual gifts are only available to born-again believers. Believers have an advantage in that the talents, strengths, or abilities that come naturally to them can be enhanced to function supernaturally or above their natural limits by the Holy Spirit (Rom. 12:6–8, 1 Cor. 12:8–10, Eph. 4:11). *See* also **Anointing; Fivefold ministry; Grace**

Glory: In the Hebrew it is the word *kabod,* meaning *weight* or *heaviness.* It also means *honour, importance,* and *majesty.* In the Greek it is the word *doxa,* which means *brightness.* The glory of God speaks about God revealing His *essence, presence, power, majesty,* or beauty to be seen, felt, and heard and not only sensed. The glory may also speak about a certain **dimension** or level where God's presence can be witnessed or sensed. This sort of atmosphere is often referred to as **open heaven**. When the glory of God is manifested, signs such as silver and gold dust, angels, angel feathers, heavenly manna, smoke, clouds, oil, creative miracles, etc., can be seen. The **shekinah glory** refers to the visible presence of God's glory, which is usually seen in a cloud of smoke (Ex. 16:7, Isa. 40:5, Hab. 2:14). Going from **glory to glory** refers to the increase of the glory **dimension** operating or present in the life of a believer. Every believer is called by God to ascend into new levels of glory (2 Cor. 3:18).

God's timing: This refers to the set time, seasons, and place in which God wants to do something through someone on the earth. The time taken to hear from God concerning His timing for a particular decision or answer is called **waiting on God / the Lord** (Ps. 37:7, Isa. 40:31, Hab. 2:3). God's timing often goes with **God's release,** which is the *peace, comfort, or leading of the Holy Spirit* indicating it is time for a believer to move in a certain direction or make certain decisions. God's timing and release are needed most by believers when making big decisions like starting a church or a business, relocating countries, marriage, etc. God's timing and His release lead to **open doors** and His **grace** (1 Sam. 30:6–8, Ps. 27:14, Eccles. 3:11, Hab. 2:3, Gal. 4:4). *See* also **Longsuffering/patience.**

Grace: This is the willingness and power of God to accomplish something for or through a believer that cannot be done by human effort. It is God doing for us what we cannot do for ourselves because He loves us. Grace is first received at salvation but grows and develops to bring the fullness of God's blessings and character within us. When grace manifests, it makes things that are usually hard to become easy. Grace can also show itself in the gifts of the Holy Spirit or in the anointing on the life of a believer. All ministries and gifts must be operated by depending or leaning on His grace. Most thesauruses would list synonyms of grace and favour that include: *excessive kindness, preferential treatment, unmerited favour, ease, goodwill, influence of God, to honour, kind act, unfair partiality, kind regard, to prefer, to aid or support, to approve.* Grace is given because of the finished work of Jesus Christ and not by our works. This is why it is called unmerited or undeserved favour. The opposite of grace is the Law, which covers at least two aspects. (1) It can mean following or observing the laws given to the Israelites by God in the Old Testament, which New Testament believers must not follow unless the New Testament allows for it. (2) It can also mean any self-imposed requirements, laws, rules, behaviour, rituals, demands, etc., that believers place on their lives in an attempt please God and receive His blessings Everything God does for and through a believer is by His grace, and this is why He gets all the glory (John 1:17, Rom. 3:24, 5:2, 20–21, 2 Cor. 12:9, Eph. 2:8–10, 2 Pet. 3:18). *See* also **Anointing; Gifts of the Spirit; Religious spirit**

H

Healing: This word is derived from the word *raphe'* in the Hebrew, and ordinarily it has the meaning of to *cure, cause to heal, repair,* and *make whole.* However, healing in the Bible can refer to the following: (1) curing a disease or wound and restoring it back to soundness or to its natural functions (Matt. 14:14, 20:34); or (2) to restore purity to a situation (2 Kings 2:21–22, 2 Chron. 7:14). This happens when God removes differences or sin to reconcile us to Him. This aspect can mean healing a breach or difference (Hos. 14:4). This type of healing, where God heals our sin, usually involves restoration to a place of prosperity. Healing through a believer is seen through the **gift of healing** given by the Holy Spirit, which involves the *supernatural intervention of God to a physical body to remove, cure, or subdue a sickness or disease and to restore the body to its original healthy condition* (1 Cor. 12:9). The Bible reveals that there is no limit to what God can cure through a believer (HIV, cancer, heart disease, broken bones, and more can all be healed). Healing often operates with signs such as **miracles, deliverance**, and **special faith** (Acts: 5:16, 10:38). Healing also covers healing of the mind, heart, and emotions. The healing of the Lord can cure fears, depression, anxiety, suicide, etc. (Rom. 12:2, Phil. 4:6–8, 1 Pet. 5:7). *See* also **Inner healing.**

Honouring leaders: This refers to the tribute, respect, and acknowledgment shown to a leader in the **body of Christ**. This can be a personal leader in the local church or a general leader in the **fivefold ministry** or seven mountain kingdoms. It can also be referred to as honouring spiritual fathers or mothers in the faith, honouring men or women of God, etc. This honour can be expressed through words, sowing, serving, submission, etc. (Gal. 6:6, 1 Thess. 5:12–13, 1 Tim. 5:17–19, Heb. 13:7). *See* also **Prophet's reward; Spiritual authority**

I

Identifying gifts and callings: This refers to the recognition and classification of the gifts of the Holy Spirit and the areas of callings God has entrusted or given to believers to enable them to function in their membership roles in the church and generally to be used by God. These gifts and callings are identified by using the prophetic gifts and observing the fruit and works in the life of a believer. Apostolic and prophetic leaders are very necessary for this process. *See* also **Calling; Gifts of the Holy Spirit; Prophetic presbytery; TEAR programme**

Intercession: This refers to the prayers of a believer or a group of believers offered on behalf of other people. Intercession can include **fasting**. Intercession can also be offered by praying in the **gift of tongues** (Rom. 8:26). Intercession is also called **standing in the gap** (Ezek. 22:30). God needs intercessors to pray for the following: (1) **For the lost,** which are the unsaved and backslidden. (2) For governments and rulers to be saved and obey the Word of God (1 Tim. 2:1–3). (3) For church leaders, the church, and believers in general to be in the perfect will of God. This includes to be strengthened, protected, provided for, etc. (Eph. 6:18, 1 Thess. 5:25, James 5:16). (4) Prayers to oppose the **kingdom of darkness** and establish the **kingdom of God** on earth. Intercession is a necessary and powerful tool for God to use to advance His Kingdom. All believers must therefore pray for others and more especially those who sense a calling for intercession. Some forms of intercession include **prayer walks** where believers walk to a particular place and intercede (Josh. 1:3) and **prayer watches,** where usually a group of believers pray for long a period of time, often in shifts or rotations (Eph. 6:18, 1 Thess. 1:2, 1 Tim. 2:1).

J

Jezebel spirit: This refers to a certain type of demonic spirit or influence. This spirit is identified according to the characteristics of Jezebel in the Bible. The Bible does not speak about a *Jezebel spirit* but about Jezebel's conduct and character. This spirit is usually identified by the following characteristics: (1) opposing God's true worship and prophetic voice; (2) manipulating high-ranking officials to oppose the gospel of Jesus Christ; (3) manipulative, controlling, and selfish behaviours; (4) **sexual immorality**; and (5) **idolatry**. *(Generally read 1 and 2 Kings, Revelation 2:18–29.)*

Journaling: This refers to the process of writing down, anything that relates to God and the life of a believer, especially in a book or journal dedicated for that purpose. They can include thoughts, ideas, psalms, poems, letters, etc. Believers must regularly use this method as a way of growing in hearing the voice of God for themselves and for others (Ps. 119:105, Hab.2:2). *See* also **Practicing the presence of God; Prophetic gifts;** *Rhema*

Joshua generation: This refers to a generation that will follow the mandate God gave to Joshua, which is known as the **Joshua assignment** or **mandate**. This mandate includes taking the land and wealth God has promised His people and destroying His and our enemies. The Joshua generation is characterized as being passionate, uncompromising, and ready to take the Promised Land. Although the Promised Land literally referred to Israel for the Jewish people, for the church it speaks about the whole earth, which is our inheritance (Deut.7:1–2, Josh.1:1–5, 21:43–45, 24:14–15).

K

Kingdom of God: Kingdom is the Greek word *basileia,* which means *royal power, kingship, dominion,* or the *right* or *authority to rule over another kingdom.* This term therefore refers to the rule or government of God on the earth seen through the believers' kingship, power, dominion, right, or **authority** given to them by the King of Kings. This kingdom can refer to two areas. (1) It can be any place where God establishes His order and His way of doing things or in other words, anywhere His rule or dominion is physically seen in any of the **seven mountain kingdoms**. (2) The kingdom can also refer to a place in the **spiritual realm** where believers function from, since we are already seated with Christ in heavenly places according to Ephesians 2:6. **Kingdom now** refers to establishing this government now before Jesus physically brings it in its fullness on the earth. **The kingdom now** and **kingdom of God movements** have been birthed from this principle (Dan. 4:3, Matt. 3:2, Luke 16:16). *See* also **New Jerusalem.**

Kings and priests: This term by the *logos* definition, refers to the state or nature of every believer given to us by Jesus as our King of kings and our High Priest. This is why the Bible calls believers royal priesthood. (1 Pet. 2:9) This king or priest position applies to both male and female. By the *rhema* meaning it refers to two categories of believers. (1) Kings are 'market' or 'secular world' based. They are believers that God has anointed to penetrate, influence and dominate the seven major areas of human life and activity (government, education, economy, family, media, religion, and arts) These believers are ministers of God just as preachers are. They are fully empowered and recognized by God. Joseph, Daniel and Esther in the Bible are examples of this type of believer. (2) The priests are mainly church based. They are believers who have been called into the fivefold offices, (**apostles, prophets, evangelists, pastors**

and **teachers**) as well as believers who serve in the local church full time without necessarily being a Fivefold minister. (Rev. 1:6; 5:10; Heb. 2:17; 4:14). The **Kings and Priests movement** is a movement dedicated to identifying, maturing and sending those called as kings and priests, in order to establish the government of God. A combination of fivefold offices plus seven areas to dominate equals the number twelve, which is the number representing the government of God. This movement when it is in full operation will usher in the **rapture** and ultimately the **second coming** of Jesus Christ. *See* also **Apostle / prophet in the market place; Fivefold ministry; Kingly believer; Who we are in Christ**

L

Latter rain: This refers to a **latter day** or **end-time** move or outpouring of the Holy Spirit, referred to as the latter rain. This outpouring will bring with it **revivals**, miracles, harvesting of souls, and **prosperity** to the church. This latter rain is distinguished from the *former rain* as a fresh way in which God is going to pour out His Spirit on the earth. The **latter rain movement** has come from this revelation. The teachings of the latter rain movement put emphasis on believers walking in the **gifts of the Spirit**, **laying on of hands, restoration** of the **fivefold ministry**, unity of the church, and so on. The latter rain revelation also refers to the **latter day saints,** which are believers who will carry and manifest this latter rain move. (*This is not to be confused with the Church of Jesus Christ of Latter-day Saints.*) (Joel 2:23, Hos. 6:3, Zech. 10:1, James 5:7.)

Laying on of hands: This refers to the act of a believer physically putting hands on someone as a **point of contact** to release faith for something to happen to or for that person. Hands can be laid on someone for healing, an **operation of the Holy Spirit, prayer, impartation, activation,** etc. (Mark 16:18, Acts 8:17, 13:3, 2 Tim. 1:6).

Logos: It is a Greek translation from *word*. The *logos* is used to refer to the canonized Scriptures as they are contained in the sixty-six books of the Bible as the ultimate and highest authority of truth on earth. The *logos* is the written Word of God (John 17:17, 2 Tim. 3:16–17, 2 Pet. 1:20–21). *See* also **Doctrine; *Rhema*; Teaching**

Love: This is the main nature and characteristic of God and should be for every believer. Love is the main **fruit of the Spirit** because the other eight find their place in love. Love is also a commandment given to all believers to walk in. Love for God (not His blessings) and His people is one of the great keys for believers to walk in the power of God in these last days (John 3:16, 15:9–17, 1 Cor. 13:4–8, Gal. 5:13, 22–23, 1 John 4:7–12). *See* also **Character.**

M

Manifest sons of God: This refers to a people God is raising to operate like Jesus did on the earth. This revelation focuses on believers seeing themselves as sons and daughters of God endued with the same Holy Spirit and the same rights as the Son of God, Jesus Christ. The **manifest sons of God movement** has come from this revelation. This movement is similar to the **latter rain movement** (John 1:12, Rom. 8:19, Gal. 3:26, 1 John 3:1). *See* also **Sons of God.**

Manifestation: This means to *reveal* or *bring out into the natural something that is in the supernatural or spiritual realm.* It can relate to the promises of God, demons, or angels. Manifestation put differently is the *seen physical evidence of the things that are unseen. See* also **Faith; Spiritual realm; Supernatural.**

Mantle: It is derived from the meaning of to *cover* as in a *blanket* or *coat*. It is an anointing that covers a believer. A mantle is unique or specific to the believer it rests upon. It cannot be shared or given while the believer is still alive or on the earth because it is what God has clothed the believer with to operate with while on earth. It is his or her personal and unique anointing, gifts, or *grace* (2 Kings 2:9–13, 13:21). Mantle can be used in some of the following ways: (1) **Placing a demand on the mantle/anointing**, which means to recognise the anointing that accompanies the mantle of another believer and by faith placing an expectation for the anointing that flows with that mantle to be released. Many people did this in the Bible and received healings and other blessings (2 Kings 2:9, Mark 5:25–34). (2) **Honouring the mantle/anointing**, which means to intentionally recognise and respect the mantle with its anointing upon another believer. This honour is expressed through words and actions that intentionally pay tribute to the man or woman of God. This can result in God releasing a blessing that is upon that mantle (2 Kings 4:8–17, Matt. 10:41–42). (3) **Taking up the mantle**, which means carrying on with the mantle of a man or woman of God from where he or she stopped on the earth. This may involve carrying on with the person's doctrine, gifts, and callings (2 Kings 2:9–15). *See* also **Honouring man and woman of God.**

Meditation: This is the process by which a believer focuses on a certain Scripture, teaching, or concept from God to get **revelation** from it and allow it to become part of his or her thinking and **faith**. To meditate put differently is to chew and digest on the Word to obtain a richer and fuller meaning from it. Instead of reading the Bible in chapters, meditation often focuses on certain verses. It is a necessary way to change the Bible from being mere information to becoming **revelation** that results in **faith** and **spiritual growth**. Meditation also results in the **renewing of the mind** of a believer. This means to change the old ways of thinking based on the flesh and the devil to begin thinking according to the thought patterns of God (Josh. 1:8, Prov. 23:7, Rom. 12:2, Phil. 4:8). *See* also **Repentance.**

Movement: This is a specific way in which the Holy Spirit moves in a certain place, time, or season with a specific set of people on earth. We can better understand a Holy Spirit–inspired movement by looking at its characteristics, which may include the following: (1) It is always initiated or started by God. God starts movements when He wants to establish certain aspects of His will or Word on earth. (2) God uses pioneers and fathers on earth to begin and nurture the movement. It may be one or several. (3) It is based on Scripture and sound doctrine. (4) It may take time to be accepted, but it eventually becomes part of the revelation caught by the general body of Christ. A movement usually has with it a large number who accept the revelation and move with it. (5) It comes with the demonstration of what it teaches. Its validity must be confirmed with manifestations. (6) It is usually followed by books, teachings, and resources to teach and clarify what the movement is about. Examples of past and present movements and the truth restored include the following: The Protestant movement, which brought restoration of salvation by grace and not through works. It opposed or protested the then long-standing Roman Catholic doctrines (hence the name *Protestant*). They were also called Lutherans (named after major pioneer Martin Luther). The **evangelical movement** brought about the emphasis on water baptism by immersion. The holiness movement brought the restoration of believers living a sanctified life (also called *Methodist* due to the methods they employed in living according to the principles they believed in). The **faith-healing movement** brought the restoration of healing as a promise for every believer. The **Pentecostal movement** brought the restoration of the experience that occurred on the day of Pentecost in Acts 2, which brought the indwelling presence of the Holy Spirit with evidence of speaking in new tongues (hence the name *Pentecostal*). The **charismatic movement** brought the restoration of the other gifts of the Spirit. (The Greek word for gifts is *charisma*, hence the term *charismatic*). The **faith movement** brought about the restoration on faith in the Word and the promises of prosperity and healing for every believer. The **prophetic movement** brought with it the restoration of the office of the prophet and the prophetic gifts. The **apostolic movement** brought the restoration of the office of the apostle and the apostolic gifts. The name of the movement should not matter as long as it is supported by the Scriptures. Some movements may have the same essential message but have different names depending on the revelation God gives to the founders or pioneers. For example the **kings and priests movement**, **dominion movement**, and **manifest sons of God movement** all emphasize believers taking over the earth for Jesus and manifesting His power and authority. Believers should not get caught up in names of movements but in the message behind them. *See* also **Present truth; Restoration.**

N

New age: This refers to the popular belief system arising in the world today based on Eastern religions and rituals. Its followers are called new agers. All new age practices emanate from **witchcraft**, the **occult,** and satan and are therefore strictly forbidden for believers. The **new age movement** has come from this concept (Deut. 18:9–12, Isa. 2:6). *See* **also Demonic/forbidden practices.**

P

Prophet's reward: This refers to a blessing or reward believers receive by honouring the mantle or anointing that is on a **prophet** of God or his or her prophecies, usually by acting on his or her word and by accepting it as a word from God (2 Chron. 20:20, Matt. 10:41). *See* also **Honouring leaders; Personal prophecy.**

Practising the presence of God: This refers to activities or exercises done by the believer to better hear and listen to the voice of God. Some of these activities include time in **prayer, meditation, praise and worship,**

journaling, etc. Every believer should be able to hear and speak the heart and mind of God (John 10:27).

R

Rapture: This refers to an event of the snatching away of the church and believers from the earth so they can meet Jesus in mid-air. The word *rapture*, which is not actually found in the English Bible, is an English word that comes from the Latin *rapiemur* or *rapere*, which means to *snatch away*. It has been translated from the Greek word *harpagisometha* or *harpaz,* which means to be *caught up.* The rapture is not the **second coming** of Christ because during the rapture, Jesus does not physically come to earth but remains mid-air, where we will be *caught up* to meet Him. The second coming is the time when Jesus comes to the earth to judge the **antichrist,** the **false prophet,** and satan and his demons and to establish His kingdom physically on the earth. There are some who believe the rapture will occur before the **great tribulation.** This theory is called **pre-tribulation rapture**. Some believe it will happen in the middle of the tribulation or in a **mid-tribulation rapture**. Some believe it will be before the wrath of Christ on the earth or in a **pre-wrath rapture**. Then there are others who believe it will be after the great tribulation or a **post-tribulation rapture**. There seem to be Scriptures to support all of these theories, and believers should make up their own minds. Regardless of the time of the rapture, all believers have a responsibility to live lives that are holy and pleasing before God to be a part of it (Matt. 24:42, 1 Cor. 15:51–52, 1 Thess. 4:16–18, 5:2,23). *See* also **Eschatology.**

Receptive to the Holy Spirit: This refers to the level of sensitivity a believer has to the communication of God given by the Holy Spirit. God is always talking to believers, and He desires for all to hear His voice and to obey it (John 10:27, 14:26, 16:12–14). *See* also **Conviction of the Holy Spirit; Yielding to the Holy Spirit.**

Restoration: This refers to when the Holy Spirit reinstates a certain scriptural truth on the earth (Acts 3:21). For example, the restoration of the prophets and the apostles means these offices are being put in their rightful position and recognition to function as God has intended. (2) Restoration can also mean when God gives back to a believer whatever has been lost, stolen, or taken by the enemy. Restoration is often given in a greater quantity and quality (Prov. 6:30–31, Joel 2:25–26, Luke 4:18–19, John 10:10). *See* also **Present truth; Third reformation.**

Revelation: This is the word *apokalupsis* in the Greek, and it means to *make bare* or to *make naked*. It also means to *appear*, to *manifest*, to be *uncovered*, or to be *unveiled*. Revelation is also called **divine revelation**. A revelation therefore means when the Holy Spirit unveils, manifests, or uncovers a particular truth in the Scripture or the **spiritual realm**. Revelation is progressive and comes in stages (Acts 26:16). The more it is pursued, the more it increases. It is the deepest and highest form of understanding God and His Word. The more time spent with a Scripture or truth, the more revelation comes from it. Revelation comes from **meditation** and brings **manifestation** (Josh 1:8–9, Mark 4:24). When a Scripture has not become revelation, it is still *information*, meaning it is in the head of a believer and not the heart or spirit. In this way it cannot be spoken and produce results. Every believer should seek to move in this dimension and trust God for regular revelation because revelation is the source of faith, and faith is the only thing God can use to bring manifestation of His Word or promises (Matt. 16:17, Rom. 10:8–10, 1 Cor. 2:10, Eph. 3:3–5). *See* also **Faith; *Rhema*.**

Revival: This refers to when the Holy Spirit awakens or makes alive either a dormant or non-existent truth in the Scriptures. The word *revive* means to *bring back to life* or to *live again*. Revivals are usually characterized by people in a certain area having a greater awareness of God followed by services, soul winning, repentance, intercession, gifts of the Spirit, and miracles. **Revivalists** are believers who pioneer or lead revivals.

Rhema: A *rhema* word is a word from God that the Holy Spirit reveals or speaks to the believer. It refers to a *word that is spoken* rather than a *word that is written*. It can also be called a **revealed word**. It is described as a *word from God* as distinguished from a *word of God* (John 14:26). A *rhema* word is similar to a revelation. A *rhema* word is usually personal whereas the *logos* is general. For example, the *logos* will tell a believer to sow financial seed, but the *rhema* will tell the believer where to sow the seed and/or what to believe God for. A *rhema* is often contained in prophecies. *See* also *Logos*; **Revelation.**

S

Salvation: This refers to the state of being saved or delivered from danger, harm, or God's wrath. When people become born again or **saved,** they enter into God's salvation. The word *salvation* is the Greek word *soteria* (taken from *sozo,* meaning *to rescue*), and it means *welfare, prosperity, deliverance, preservation,* and *safety.* God's salvation covers every area of life and not only taking the believer to heaven (Luke 19:9, Acts 4:12, Rom. 10:9–10). *See* also **Born again; Sinner's prayer.**

School of the fivefold ministries: These are schools set up to teach, train, activate, and release fivefold ministers into the body of Christ. Some may have names like **school of the prophets** or **school of the apostles** (Eph. 4:11). *See* also **Fivefold ministry.**

School of the Holy Spirit: These are schools that seek to manifest the **gifts of the Spirit** through the students they teach. They can also be called **school of the Spirit, training centres,** etc. They are different from ordinary Bible schools and seminaries because they emphasise demonstrating the power they are teaching and teach their students how to do the same (1 Cor. 2:4). *See* also **Demonstrations of the Holy Spirit;, TEAR programme.**

Seeking the face/heart of God: This refers to a type of heartfelt prayer and meditation that looks for the guidance, peace, and presence of God. This type of prayer is *intimate, intense, honest,* and from the deepest part of the believer. This type of prayer can be contrasted with **seeking the hand of God**, which is the type of prayers and attitude focused on needs and wants without the desire to connect to God through genuine love and devotion for Him (1 Chron. 16:11, 22:19, Ps. 27:4, 8, Isa. 55:6, James 4:8). *See* also **Praise and worship; Prayer of consecration.**

Seven mountain kingdoms: This refers to the seven major areas of activity, life, or **spheres of influence** on the earth. They consist of: (1) *government and law;* (2) *education;* (3) *economy (business and finance);* (4) *family;* (5) *media and communication;* (6) *religion (spirituality and church);* and (7) *arts* and *entertainment.* According to the **seven mountain mandate,** all of these areas must be penetrated, influenced, and dominated by the **kingdom of God** through believers before Jesus Christ returns (Gen. 1:26–27, Deut. 7:1–2, Matt. 5:13–16, Luke 10:19, 1 John 5:19). *See* also **end-time transfer of wealth, Joshua generation, kings.**

Signs and wonders: This refers to any *unusual, uncommon,* or *unnatural* manifestations that happen through the presence and power of God. Signs and wonders are not limited and can mean any way in which God wants to reveal Himself. They are limitless because God is limitless. This term speaks about anything that makes people stand in awe or wonder of God. The main reason for these signs and wonders is for the unsaved to be convinced Jesus is who He says He is. Examples of signs and wonders include people being **slain in the Spirit**, the glory of God manifesting, miracles, etc. It can also include **healings, deliverance,** and **creative miracles** (Mark 16:20, John 21:25, Heb. 2:4). *See* also **Demonstrations of the Holy Spirit; Power evangelism/ witnessing.**

Sons of God: This refers to the position believers have been given by God as sons and daughters of God. It is a position of **sonship.** It relates to the Father-and-child relationship each believer has with God. Sonship has *nothing to do with gender, race, or age.* Just as Jesus has this relationship with the Father, even so all believers are called sons of God. This is a position of inheritance that all believers enjoy in the kingdom of God. We have been given the right to share in all things with Jesus Christ; this is why the Bible also refers to believers as **heirs** and **joint or co-heirs** with Christ (Rom. 8:17). There are two words translated as sons in the New Testament. (1) There is the word, *technon,* that refers to infant, child, or youth, and (2) *hoius,* which speaks about one grown or developed into maturity. *Hoius* is the type of son God is seeking to raise as the manifest sons of God. Believers who fail to appropriate the truth of sonship suffer from an **orphan spirit/mind-set.** This type of thinking is a **stronghold** of the devil that prevents believers from realising their adoption to God the Father (Gal. 4:6–7, 1 John 3:1–2). *See* also **Fatherhood; Manifest sons of God.**

Spiritual authority: This refers to the people God has placed over others by virtue of their position and offices in the local church and in the body of Christ. **Submission to spiritual authority** refers to the decisions and actions taken by believers to obey, serve, and promote the interests and instructions of those in spiritual authority over them. *See* also **Apostolic and prophetic order; Elders; Fivefold ministry; Spiritual parents.**

Spiritual mentoring: This refers to the process of providing guidance and grooming by a spiritual elder to another to shape and develop the learner into what God has called him or her to be. This type of mentoring is based on a relationship that involves a mentor using the principles of the

Word of God to give direction to those under him or her. This process can also be called **discipling / discipleship** (Prov. 27:17, 2 Tim. 2:2, Titus 2:3-5). *See* also **Fatherhood; Spiritual parents; Training.**

Spiritual realm: This refers to the unseen world that coexists with the natural world where angels, demons, and God live. It can also be called the **realm of the Spirit**. There are three main levels that are recognized in the spiritual realm. The first is from beneath the earth to the sky. The second is between the sky we see and heaven or outer space. The third and highest realm is heaven, where God and His angels dwell. The realm of the Spirit is accessed through faith in God or through fear in the lies of the devil. Believers can bring the manifestation of their faith or their fears, depending on which voices they are listening to in the spiritual realm (Acts 1:9–11, Eph. 1:3, 6:12). *See* also **Angelic ministry; Faith; satan/demons.**

Spiritual warfare: This refers to the battle that takes place in the **spiritual realm** between the **kingdom of darkness** and God, His angels, and believers. Believers have been equipped with the armour of God, which includes the following (Eph. 6:11–18): (1) truth of the Bible; (2) righteousness found in Christ Jesus; (3) readiness to preach the gospel of Jesus Christ; (4) faith in God; (5) salvation; (6) Word of God; (7) and prayers and supplication in the Spirit. Believers have also been equipped with **weapons of warfare** found in God (1 Cor. 10:4–5). These include: (1) **prayer;** (2) **pleading the blood of Jesus Christ;** (3) **angelic ministry;** (4) **fasting;** and (5) **speaking the Word.**

Supernatural: This means to be or being *above* and *beyond* that which is natural. It also means *abnormal* or *extraordinary*. It refers to that which cannot be understood or explained by natural reasoning and human wisdom. *Natural* is defined as in conformity with the ordinary course of nature, not unusual or exceptional, or that which can be experienced by the five senses, understood by the mind, or explained by human reasoning. Although this definition focuses on the supernatural as given by God, it is important to note that there are *two sources* of the supernatural. It may come from **satan** and his **demons**, often seen in **magic, witchcraft,** or **sorcery** (Acts 8:9–11, 16:16–19, 2 Cor. 11:14) and in other **false religions.** The other source is God working through the Holy Spirit and the Word. The believer must ensure to always seek the true source of the supernatural, which is God. The **anointing** or **gifts of the Holy Spirit** and **grace** are all supernatural because all of them come from God's ability in us and none of our own abilities. **Releasing the supernatural** refers to any action of faith followed by a physical manifestation done by a believer to demonstrate the power of the Holy Spirit. **Activating the supernatural** refers to the stirring up of the **gifts of the Holy Spirit** within the believer so he or she will outwardly or physically display this supernatural power of God. This outward display of the power of Holy Spirit is also called **walking in the supernatural power of God**. *See* also **Demonstrations of the Holy Spirit; Miracles; Spiritual realm.**

T

TEAR programme: This acronym stands for training by equipping, activating, and releasing. It is premised or based on the mandate given in Ephesians 4:11–16 for the fivefold ministry. The focus of this programme is to train all believers by equipping them with the truth of their calling and the gifts on their lives, by using both the *logos* and *rhema* Word of God. This process of **equipping** involves a lot of teaching from the Bible and prophecies over a believer. The next step is **activation,** which involves activating or imparting the gifts and calling on the person being trained by the trainer. The last step is **releasing** the believer to walk in these gifts and callings and for the believer to then train, equip, activate, and release other believers. This is a continual process until all saints are perfected. *See* also **Fivefold ministry; Training; School of the Spirit.**

V

Visitation: This refers to the manifestation of an angel or God appearing to a human being. Visitations are called such because generally angels and God live in the **spiritual realm** and not in the natural realm. Demonic visitations cannot be regarded as falling within this definition because they are unwanted and unwelcome and generally have no right to be near or around believers unless given permission. Visitations can come through or in the form of **dreams**, **visions**, **trances,** or actual manifestation while a believer is in his or her natural state of body and mind (Luke 1:26–37, Acts 10:3–7, 27:23–24, Heb. 13:2). *See* also **Angelic ministry.**

Wilderness experience/period: This refers to a period of time in a believer's life that brings with it trials and challenging situations. This term can more commonly be used to mean a period of preparation and testing by God. It is not uncommon for believers to experience this period before God releases a **breakthrough** (Deut. 8:2–3, Matt. 4:1–11). *See* also **Preparation of man/woman of God; Season; Trials/ tests/ tribulations/ sufferings.**

Winning souls: This refers to witnessing or telling unbelievers about the cross of Jesus Christ and then leading them to salvation through prayer. This is also called leading people into salvation, **soul winning,** or **winning the lost**. Wining souls is the primary duty of every believer (Prov. 11:30, Matt. 28:19). *See* also **Born again; End-time transfer; Great Commission; Power evangelism/witnessing; Salvation; Sinner's prayer.**

Word of knowledge: This refers to when Holy Spirit reveals the *past* or *present* facts about a person, place, or situation. It may include names, numbers, or any other information. It is different from human knowledge because the information that comes is unknown to the person giving it until God reveals it (2 Kings 5:26, John 4:17–18). *See* also **Prophetic gifts.**

Word of wisdom: This refers to when the Holy Spirit reveals the *guidance* and *direction* needed to solve a particular problem. It is a God-inspired way to solve problems. It is different from human wisdom because the word of wisdom comes directly from God to solve a problem and not from the natural mind. God usually reveals a situation through the **word of knowledge** and then gives the solution through a word of wisdom (Gen. 41:34–35). *See* also **Prophetic gifts.**

Y

Yielding to the Holy Spirit: This may also be called **submitting to the Holy Spirit,** and it refers to the voluntary decision and action of faith a believer makes to allow the Holy Spirit to lead, direct, and flow through him or her. This is what is referred to as **walking in the Spirit**. Believers must make an effort to regularly *invite* the Holy Spirit to manifest His nature, His gifts, and His fruit in their lives. This will also result in the **leading of the Holy Spirit** or being **Spirit led**, which essentially is the direction given to a believer in matters of life by the Holy Spirit (Isa. 11:1–2, Gal. 5:16, 22–23). *See* also **Fruit of the Spirit: Seven spirits of God.**

Z

Zoe: This is the Greek word for *life*, which refers to *the life of God.* The zoe life is the very life that God is and has to give away. God is self-existent and needs no other source to keep Him alive because He is life itself. He is the fullness of life. Believers have access to this life, and by keeping and speaking the Word, they can life to anGod permits (John 1:4, 10:10, 14:6).

BIBLIOGRAPHY AND RECOMMENDED READING

Abraham S. Rajah, *Apostolic & Prophetic Dictionary*. Johannesburg, South Africa: Trumpet Publications, 2013.

Bill Hamon, *Apostles Prophets and the Coming Moves of God*.: Shippensburg, PA: Destiny Image Publications, 1997.
Prophets and the Prophetic Movement. Shippensburg, PA: Destiny Image, 1990

C. Peter Wagner, *Discover Your Spiritual Gifts*. Ventura, California U.S.A.: Regal Books, 2005.

John Eckhardt, *God Still Speaks*: Charisma House, Lake Mary Florida, 2009.
Ordinary People Extraordinary Power: Charisma House, Lake Mary Florida, chapter 10, 2010.

Jonathan David, *Moving in the Gifts of Revelation & Prophecy*. Johor, Malaysia Destiny Heights, 1993.

Jonathan Welton, *The School of the Seer*. Shippensburg, PA: Destiny Image, 2009.

Kenneth E. Hagin, *The Holy Spirit and His Gifts*. Tulsa, OK: Faith Library Publications, 1991.

Patricia King, *Light Belongs in the Darkness*. Shippensburg, PA: Destiny Image, chapter 5, 2005.

Paula A. Price, *The Prophets Dictionary*. New Kensington PA: Whitaker Publications, 2006.

ABOUT THE AUTHOR

Abraham S. Rajah has been raised by God to father and pioneer the *kings and priests movement,* which includes the restoration of the apostolic and prophetic ministry.

The *priests* restoration is focused on identifying, training, and maturing those called into the fivefold ministry (*apostles, prophets, evangelists, pastors, and teachers*) to bring every believer to fulfil his or her role in the body of Christ. The *kings* restoration is focused on raising believers who are called to exert dominion over the seven spheres of influence: *government, education, economy, family, media, religion,* and *arts.*

He has been graced by God to walk in the office of the apostle, prophet, and teacher. His mandate from God includes raising and activating every believer to walk in his or her calling and in the supernatural power of God evidenced by the gifts of the Holy Spirit, in signs, wonders, and miracles.

This mandate has been prophesied many times over his life.

As a result of this mandate, the Holy Spirit and he have developed the *TEAR* programme (training by equipping, activating, and releasing) with books and manuals.

He completed his diploma at Heritage of Faith Bible Institute of Jerry Savelle Ministries.

He is the apostle and founder of Kings and Priests International (*KPI*), a network of churches and ministries. The mantra of *KPI* is summed up in these words: *preparing every nation for Kingdom demonstration.*

He is also the founder of the Kings and Priests Movement Church

(*KPMC*). The church is dedicated to the calling and mandate of kings and priests.

He is married to a lovely wife, Hephzibah. Both of them have law degrees and have a number of years in private legal practice. They run *KPI* and *KPMC* together.

They have three children—a daughter, Abigail, and two sons, Elijah and Zion Abraham, who stay with them in Johannesburg, South Africa, which is also the headquarters of their international ministry.

BECOME A PARTNER TODAY!

Help Kings and Priests International (*KPI*) take this final move of God around the world.

What Is a KPI Partner?

- A partner is anyone who makes a decision to support this ministry in finances, prayer, and fasting. (The vision of the ministry is on the website for prayer and fasting.)
- We at *KPI* believe your tithes belong to your local church.

Why Partner with KPI?

- As much as God has given this ministry this unique and extremely important vision, it cannot be done without your help and support. God wants to restore His church to a place of power and dominion and for His people to move in signs, wonders, and mirales aswe embrace the apostolic and prophetic movement.
- *KPI* is dedicated to producing books, CD's, DVD's, and manuals and building training centres in Africa and around the world to see the rise of God's kings and priests (Rev. 5:11).
- We believe your financial needs will be met. We trust God for debt cancellations, business ideas, approved loans, etc.

- We believe God will pour on you the signs, wonders, and gifts that move with the apostolic and prophetic ministry we are (Gal. 6:6–9, Matt. 10:41, Phil. 4:16–18, 2 Kings 4:4–18).
- You get exclusive invites to partner gathering, complete with personal prophecies and prayer.
- Not to mention free materials and resources as they become available.

How to Partner with KPI

You can partner financially with *KPI* in the following ways:
- Direct bank deposit
- Electronic or wire transfer (EFT)
- Debit or stop order
- Cheques (written out to Kings and Priests International)

When to Partner with KPI

- This is between you and God. However, we encourage you to make a prayerful decision to become a *monthly partner* with us. No amount is too small or too big.
- If the Lord has laid it in your heart to sow into *KPI* land, houses, vehicles, jewellery, furniture, etc., please contact us to arrange for the logistics.

Partnership information can be found on our website. www.kingspriests. co.za.

CONTACT INFORMATION

To order more copies of *this book,* or other books, please visit our website for more information at www.kingspriests.co.za or e-mail info@ kingspriests.co.za.

Call centre +27 11 056 5822 /+27 82 2290 370
SMS +27 82 2290 370

Or you can write to us at:

P.O. Box 783153
Sandton
2146
Johannesburg
South Africa

Kings and Priests are social. Are you?

Facebook: apostle&prophetabrahamsrajah
Twitter: @kingspriests
Youtube

INVITATIONS

To invite the author to preach or teach at your local church, conference, or Bible school. Pease visit us at *www.kingspriests.co.za* and click on *Invitation* on the home page, or use the contact information provided.

WALKING THIS JOURNEY WITH YOU

Send us your deepest prayer request now! Precious believer, my wife, Prophetess Hephzibah, and I want to stand with you for your most *urgent needs*. Whether you need breakthrough in finances, marriage, demonic oppression, depression, direction, or anything else—*we mean anything*—send your prayer request via our many social applications on prayer@kingspriests.co.za

Don't forget to send us your testimony. We know God will do something amazing in your life once we release our faith together.

We love you and wait to hear from you.